Teacher

D0319357

H46 380 549 0

Also available from Continuum

9 Habits of Highly Effective Teachers, Jacquie Turnbull
Not Quite a Teacher, Tom Bennett
Pimp your Lesson!, Isabella Wallace and Leah Kirkman
The Behaviour Guru, Tom Bennett
The Ultimate Teaching Manual, Gererd Dixie

Teacher

Mastering the Art and Craft of Teaching

TOM BENNETT

continuum

Continuum International Publishing Group

The Tower Building	80 Maiden Lane
11 York Road	Suite 704
London SE1 7NX	New York NY 10038

www.continuumbooks.com

© Tom Bennett, 2012

Illustrations © Tom Bennett, 2012

All rights reserved. No part of this publication may be reproduced or transmitted in any form or by any means, electronic or mechanical, including photocopying, recording, or any information storage or retrieval system, without prior permission in writing from the publishers.

Tom Bennett has asserted his right under the Copyright, Designs and Patents Act, 1988, to be identified as Author of this work.

British Library Cataloguing-in-Publication Data
A catalogue record for this book is available from the British Library.

ISBN: 978-1-4411-1435-8 (paperback)
     978-1-4411-3782-1 (ePub)
     978-1-4411-7671-4 (PDF)

Library of Congress Cataloging-in-Publication Data
Bennett, Tom, 1971-
  Teacher : mastering the art and craft of teaching / Tom Bennett.
     p. cm.
  Includes bibliographical references and index.
  ISBN 978-1-4411-1435-8 -- ISBN 978-1-4411-3782-1 -- ISBN 978-1-4411-7671-4
1. Teaching. 2. Teachers. 3. Teachers--Great Britain. 4. Teaching--Great
Britain. I. Title.

  LB1025.3.B462 2012
  371.102--dc23

2011042821

Typeset by Fakenham Prepress Solutions, Fakenham, Norfolk NR21 8NN
Printed and bound in India

Contents

Introduction   1

Section One: What Does it Mean to Be a Teacher?   5

1   What is a Teacher?   7
2   A Brief History of Teachers   27
3   How Policy is Made   51
4   Get Me to the Greeks – The Philosophy of Teaching   61

Section Two: The Qualities of a Great Teacher –
Developing Your Teaching Character   69

5   I am the Law – Justice   71
6   Lion Taming – Courage   79
7   I am Waiting – Patience   95
8   Knowing Yourself – Wisdom   105
9   Love Your Neighbour as Yourself – Compassion   117
10   The Vices of the Profession   127

Section Three: The Workout   135

11   Harder; Better; Faster; Stronger   139
12   Working on Your Courage   147
13   Building Up Your Patience   157
14   Other Workouts   163
15   Keeping in Shape: Perpetual Professional Development
and Following the Right Career Path   185

Conclusion   199
References and Further Reading   201
Index   203

Acknowledgements

No man is an island: these are the bridges that prevent me from being, at the least, a peninsula:

Melanie Wilson and Rosie Pattinson at Continuum, Gail Robinson, Magda Wood, Michael Shaw, Aimee Fagin, Beverley Smith, Julia Rontree and Claire Bidwell at the magnificent TES, David Bridges at Wellington, my lovely correspondents and colleagues on the interweb, forums and blog, all my colleagues and students at Raines' Foundation School, who inspire and give me a reason to get out of bed every day, and most of all – of course – my family: Tam and Betty Bennett, Anthony, Hannah, Florence, Alice and Gracie. And especially Anna, who is the rock upon which I have built my church.

Tom Bennett

Introduction

If you're a teacher, you should want to be a better teacher: I like to get my values out in the open and expose my assumptions to daylight and oxygen so that they either bloom like ragwort or get eaten by bees.[1]

On *The Times Educational Supplement* Behaviour forum and in my previous books I have written about how teachers should act and respond to the thousands of questions and challenges that teachers face every day in contemporary classrooms. Many of them are similar; none of them are identical, because no situation is identical. Gradually it became obvious to me that there was a significant gap in teacher training, that many, perhaps most teachers lack training in….how to *be* a good teacher. Oh, there is a plethora of sources, texts, seminars and INSET that tells teachers what they must do, but almost nothing about what a good teacher *is*; what you must *be* in order to be a good teacher. And that's odd, because when you're asked to describe someone, you rarely say, 'Oh, he's the guy that tells the truth.' No; you say, 'He's honest.' So what is a good teacher like, other than what they do? There's a similar odd pause that many of us are familiar with, normally encountered when we meet someone for the first time. 'And what do you do?' we ask, as if all that we were could be described in the movements of our bodies.

My response is this book. My aim (and here's my overt agenda, shoved, blinking into the daylight like Terry Waite) is to help teachers to consider what they might have to become if they want to improve the kind of teacher they are. In the process my hope is that this will lead to better teaching, better learning, happier students and teachers, and ultimately a stronger profession.

Because that's what we are: professionals. Not delivery boys for foppish politicians or fashionable educational theorists. We are the

---

[1] Do bees eat?

guardians of past experience, the ones who teach; we are the ones in the classroom with the children, dodging spitballs and trying to inspire. Nobody else does it. Everyone else – the managers, the borough liaisons, the men in committees and the people who write to the papers – are peripheral. We are the ones who walk into the room when everyone else is walking out; we talk and listen and teach and learn, and there is no barrier between us and the people we lead. We always command from the front, because there is nowhere else to go.

So I've devised a way that teachers can improve at what they do by focusing on improving who they are. The first section of this book explores what it means to be a good teacher; the second part discusses the kinds of qualities that you need to improve in order to get better as a teacher. The third section will suggest the exercises that you might think about tackling in order to become a better teacher.

In the first chapter I'll explore what being a good teacher means, what the aims of education are, and what they should be. I'll also look at some very bad aims of education, many of which you'll be very familiar with. This chapter deals with the notion of what teaching is, what it should be, and what it definitely should not be.

In Chapter two I briefly explore the history of education in the UK (and beyond), because without a sense of where we've come from, our shared history, we can never appreciate where we are now... and what we need to be. It is amazing how few teachers have little appreciation of the long, long history of their profession; I believe that without awareness of our shared history, we're doomed to make the same mistakes – and we are, we are.

Who decides how schools are run? Teachers don't get to do as they please, so next we don green masks and scrub in for the nativity of policy-making, the guidance and directives that determine how education takes place in the United Kingdom, and we will scrutinize where the clouds come from that generate the rain that annually drenches us. Then I discuss problems with this approach, and the limitations of social science to provide meaningful empirical data, and how this has affected both the way we now teach and how we view our roles as teachers, in the UK and abroad.

In Section Two, we start to look at some of the philosophy that we can take into the classroom; teaching is both an art and a craft, and if we're to get better at what we should be doing, it's valuable to take a broad view of this. Luckily, there is an approach to being a good professional that dates back to the ancient Greeks: virtue ethics, expounded by, among others, Aristotle and Plato. I discuss just enough to understand why being a good teacher can mean more than just doing as you're told, and how this approach can revolutionize your teaching, the way you see yourself, and your attitude towards the profession.

Next we look at some of the qualities that a good teacher needs to have, illustrated by a selection of real life stories from myself and others that illustrate the points; in the interests of entertainment I'll keep these as humiliating as possible, because I am expert in pretending that things happened to other people.

Finally I look at some of the ways that you focus on improving these virtues in your own teaching persona, and how to make sure that your teaching persona and you real persona neither jar nor gel too much; you don't want to be able to switch off, but at the same time you need to be able to bring enough of yourself into the room in order to make the role meaningful.

There is nothing more satisfying than this job; nothing. This isn't a burden – it's a privilege. What other job provides such a series of challenges, pitted against such an extent of enormous emotional and intellectual reward? It's not a 13-week holiday jolly, nor is it a forty year slide to retirement; it's an adventure every day, if you understand who you are, what your role is, and why you are so very, very important. If I can help you in this mission then I reckon I can live with that.

This book is about becoming a better teacher. Good luck.

Tom Bennett

Section One: What Does it Mean to Be a Teacher?

1   What is a Teacher?

'IT'S TOO MUCH, ISN'T IT?'

Most people enter the teaching profession with only an intuitive understanding about what being a teacher actually is. This is understandable, but prone to pitfalls, because those tiny assumptions take root and grow into giant beanstalks throughout your career. Or worse, someone will tell you which seeds are the right ones, and if you're not careful, your garden is full of...I don't know, banana trees or something.

If you're a teacher, you need to take a step back and ask some of the most basic questions about what it is that you *actually* do – and then assess if it's what you think being a teacher is really about. So what is a teacher? It seems to me that we won't get anywhere trying to be a better one if we don't know what we mean by a teacher in the first place. If you don't know where you're going, then any road will take you there.

What is a teacher?

Possibility 1: Someone who teaches.
Think you're clever, eh? Not so fast. We've only shifted the question back a bit. What is teaching?

Possibility 2: Someone employed by a school to stand in a classroom and…you know, do the thing.
This definition at least has the benefit of being concrete and definable. You are a teacher if someone provides you with a pay cheque to teach. You turn up, make educational jazz hands, and at the end of the day you go home to a pile of marking. Children vaguely address you as Sir or Miss (or, if you're in a progressive hell-hole, 'Jim'). The problem then is that you've also simply pushed the definition back a degree, on to the shoulders of the people who employ you. How do *they* know what teaching is? What if different schools have different ideas about what a teacher is? No good.

Perhaps a better, less abstract method is to ask, 'What does a teacher seek to achieve?' The obvious answer is to say 'learning'. And then we ask, in full Socratic style, 'What is learning?' And if you thought things were vague before, we're about to press *Turbo*. Learning is another impossibly thick concept, i.e. it contains so many possible concepts and meanings that it could almost – almost – point to anything.

When we lick a battery we learn something; when we memorise a list of bones, we learn something; the first time someone breaks your heart, we learn something.[1] But surely this is an impossibly broad range of learning activities? The focus of this book is on the idea of a teacher as a professional, not in the broadest sense. What do teachers teach *in schools*? This is where the majority of teachers operate. There are also an enormous number of home tutors and educators, parents involved in home teaching, coaches, mentors and various

---

[1] Chiefly, to spurn humanity forever and live like the Mole Man.

role models. They all have something in common. So I'll give you my answer about what a teacher is…

A teacher is a professional who educates.
Let me analyze this innocent phrase. By professional, I mean a lot; I mean that it isn't just a job; it isn't something you clock on, mess about for a few hours and clock off again. This is important; like it or not, you operate in a very precious space: other people's lives. You are a small but important link on the enormous chains that comprise other people's lives. It's closer to a vocation than a job; it takes heart, passion, guts and steel, knowledge and wisdom. It's far too important not to care about. There are certainly people who *think* it is a job; it's a huge sector, and a huge number of people are required to staff it – about 1.2 million people in the UK alone put 'Teacher' on the census. You can dream on if you think they're all The Knights of the Round Table. There are turkeys in this job, just like there are turkeys everywhere.

What are the aims of education?

Let me answer this by, annoyingly, sticking my boot into the question itself, and seeing what shape remains. Education has no aims. Education is an abstract. *People* have aims. A better way to answer this question would be, then, to say, *What are the aims of people who educate?* This is much easier to answer, because we can simply make a historical survey of what humanity has done previously, and then make a judgment.

Of course this leads us to another problem: just because we can understand what the aims of people are, or have been, in education, this doesn't answer the question of what the aims of education *should* be. That's a moral question, and one very much dependent on our values and ethics. And it's one we'll explore later on. Perhaps you already have an answer in mind.

Some possible aims of education

1. **To produce a workforce that meets the needs of society**. Not a very sexy ambition, to be fair, but at least it benefits from the virtue of simplicity. Society needs plumbers, airline pilots, lawyers and carpenters – so we design schools that will meet those educational needs.

Of course, one drawback with this model is that it has a depressing emphasis on utility – what is needed, what is useful. So that's philosophy, arts and sandpits right out the window. Of course, you could argue that there is a need in society for entertainment, and people to provide it, therefore people to write, dance, sing and perform, but that's a fairly mean perspective from which to justify the arts and humanities. And it writes off enormous fields of human endeavour that we unaccountably, perhaps irrationally, are quite proud of, like Mozart, Shakespeare, you know, all that rubbish.

2. **To socialize people into the cultural values of society.**
The problem is that this aim, like many fuzzy ideas that lack specificity, means so much that it starts to mean nothing. Is it the job of education to instil the values of society? Even if we accept this axiom, the next question is, which ones? Even in Amish villages we can find dispute and subtlety of value. And a further problem is that teachers are not neutral umpires in this process; if we see education as the process where we formally instil values into children, then we encounter the problem that the teacher might very well have values of his own. You don't have to go very far to find points of disagreement between people, even people who broadly share many values. How is a Catholic teacher to act if he is expected to teach how to put on a condom? How is an atheist teacher to react to the suggestion that children in his classroom will be expected to hear a prayer, led by him, every morning?[2]

You can't just teach them values, not overtly. Despite a succession of well meaning governments, who have all seen the school system as the answer to the problems of society, children remain resolutely defiant of being told what to value. Perhaps it has something to do with how they are brought up at home? Just a thought.[3]

3. **To develop their emotional intelligence.**
This is a more modern aim, and usually involves pitfalls and conceptual mantraps similar to those found in (2) above. Emotional intelligence is so popular these days, I fully expect it to start Twittering and overtake Stephen Fry. But what does it even mean? I've looked extensively into it, and I can report back, happily, that the answer is – very little. How can emotions

---

[2] I suspect he would be hopping up and down.
[3] Crazy idea, I know.

be intelligent? How can feelings be reasonable? And by whose judgment?

Besides which, even if emotional intelligence was actually something real (which it isn't) the problem remains; how would we teach it? I don't know much about you, but I have a degree in Philosophy with Politics, which gives me a reasonable claim to expertise in those fields. What do I know about helping children to get in touch with their emotions and hug their inner child? Answer: none. I'm not a psychologist. A little learning, in this case, is certainly a dangerous thing, and brave indeed is the man or woman who dares to try to formally play games with anyone's noodles.

4. **To make them happy.**

That's nice, isn't it? And it sounds good, until you consider that nobody is actually seriously suggesting that education should be about making people unhappy. If it does, then that's incidental. Besides, the difficulty of actually trying to define happiness is so enormous, so Leviathan, that it's almost pointless even trying, and certainly too conceptually abstract to develop anything like a teaching system that could be rolled out to millions of educational professionals. Another problem is that happiness means so many things to different people. Some people get their kicks from writing furious anonymous replies on educational blogs;[4] some people read *Heat*; some people collect stamps.

A further, even less appetizing idea that has crept into schools since the 'Every Child Matters' initiative (of which more later) is the idea that teachers must actively try to make sure that students enjoy lessons. Again, while this sounds a perfectly innocent aim, it isn't, because every time a student claims that they didn't enjoy the lesson, the teacher is to be blamed. And as I'll expand upon a little later, sometimes education just isn't a blast. Sometimes it's hard; sometimes it's dry. Boo-hoo-hoo.

5. **To develop their potential.**

This is another idea that sounds lovely, mainly because it's so vague that it can mean whatever you want it to mean. The idea that we should discover what a child enjoys, what he or she is talented at, and then encourage them to blossom like little tulips is very attractive, and to be fair, it has a lot of strengths. I would certainly argue that we are usually good at the things we enjoy; perversely enough, we also seem to enjoy the things we are good

---

4 Bastards.

at. Surely this then should be the goal of education, leading intuitively as it does to the idea of happiness, fulfilment, and hopefully lifelong success?

Well, perhaps, perhaps. And I would certainly give a cautious slow handclap to this idea. But there are other things to consider: this indicates that students shouldn't be made to do anything that doesn't interest them, or that they feel uncomfortable with. But education must be more than simply allowing children to study what they want, because there are many fields and areas of knowledge that at first we might be uncertain about, until a passion develops further down the line. Or, more significantly, we might still make a claim that there are things that everyone should study, even if the student doesn't like them. Maths, for instance. Learning isn't *all* about child-driven interests, or our perception of their personal flourishing.

It certainly can include that as a subsidiary aim. But it cannot be the direct focus of education, because for a start, how on earth are we meant to divine the flourishing of anyone else, when it is so hard to discern it in ourselves? I suppose I must be one of the luckiest men in the world, because I have found a field – education – that I love so much that I would give an arm to stay within it. By that I don't suppose to claim expertise (beyond what I need to perform my role reasonably) but that I love my job, I love teaching, and I genuinely wake up every morning glad to go into school. I couldn't say that when I was running nightclubs in Soho.[5]

No, this aim of education leaves us exposed to justified allegations of tyranny – which is ironic when you consider that, on the face of it, this aim seems to be entirely composed of concern for the child's well-being. It isn't – it's fool's gold.

Where are we now?

I've briefly knocked a few tin cans from the wall. What are we left with? The answer is ancient, and yet frighteningly modern:

◆ The aim of education is to pass on to our children the very best of what humanity has already learned.

---

[5] For a start, I rarely woke up in the morning.

I'll let that sink in. Our society has evolved for thousands of years. In that time, people have been looking at the world, at themselves, and trying to understand what it all means, what we mean, questions of ultimate issues, questions of practical importance. Why are we here? What time is dinner? Can I have chips with that? Do these chaps make my bum look big?[6]

The reason we don't have perpetually to re-invent wheels or work out the best material for the filament of light bulbs is because someone has already discovered it. Helpfully, they taught others, or wrote it down. Then successive generations have run with the idea, tried to improve upon it.

This applies not only to matters scientific and practical, but to culture and art; we create, we entertain, we question, we discuss, we challenge, we interact in a million different art forms and media, and the legacy of those conversations is the inheritance of our successors. Whatever you might think about the Human Race (and the jury is still out on whether Noah's Ark could have ridden a little higher in the water), we are *jolly* inventive. We've done a lot; we've learned a lot. Many paths have been walked by those who have gone before.

But this legacy is fragile. When the barbarians were busy burning down the libraries of Alexandria, a blow was struck to civilization that didn't stop bleeding until the Renaissance, centuries later. Knowledge only exists as long as someone knows it. Oh, we can record what we have learned by a number of methods, but physical objects are even more fragile records of posterity. As soon as a fact, a skill is forgotten then someone has to rediscover it, all over again. Civilization isn't static; it's in a constant process of dynamic re-invention – every fifty years or so, a new generation comes along that has to be taught the history, the songs of the tribe; the best way to skin a calf; the best way to notch an arrow; the best way to calibrate a dampening valve for a nuclear turbine. In a world of uncertainty, I can offer this reassuring homily: in a hundred years, you will almost certainly be dead.

And this is the aim of education: the maintenance of the cultural and scientific legacy of our species; to enable nothing less than the continuation of Homo sapiens, and at least allow for the possibility that we might progress, or at the very least perpetuate. We exist, perpetually, on a cliff edge of extinction. Many people have offered artistic interpretations of post-apocalyptic scenarios, usually for our vicarious entertainment; films about nuclear war, ecological

---

6 Correct answer: no, your **enormous ass** makes it looks big.

disasters, virus outbreaks, of societal cataclysms of overpopulation, energy deprivation, hunger and want. While these are usually hyperbolic, they express a universal truth: we keep moving or we die. We take the best of what we have learned in our short lifespans, we add it to the accumulated wisdom, misery and endeavour of our ancestors, and we pass it on.

That's education. That, at its heart, is the role of the teacher. We teach students the legacy of the past, and then we pass the buck to them. It's a huge responsibility. We save the world – we create it – one person at a time.

Of course, there are many who disagree, who feel that the aims of education should be one of the possibilities suggested above. For example, they often claim that the duty of the teacher is to inspire. The question is; can we teach it? And the answer has to be no. Not directly.

This assertion will make some pop a vein: of course it can be taught, they will claim. And I would reply with qualified warmth; it can indeed be taught: individually, spontaneously, in the unique synergy between student and teacher that often occurs in the most surprising of places. The aimless bully who sees that other people can feel pain; the rudderless genius who discovers that poetry has the power to transform their life; the mute nerd who learns they have a voice. These are all common memes in fiction; of course they are – stories where people have been inspired and transformed are in themselves often transformative and inspirational. Such things do happen in real life: I am honoured to have been part of some stories like this, and moments such as these stay with you forever. And in no small measure, they play a significant part of why teaching is, I believe, the best job in the world.

But can these experiences be taught formally? No: there is no curriculum in existence that can guarantee such Damascene content; no teaching style that reliably leads to an epiphany; no qualification that could be required to contain consistent evidence of transfiguration.

Can these experiences be assessed? No: they, like much of human experience, defy classification. They are personal, intimate, unique and often inexplicable; impossible to convey or replicate. When we train, lead, educate, we must never lose sight of the fact that we are working with people, not crash-test dummies, and unlike them we flinch, anticipate, exacerbate and confound predictive measures.

Can sentiments be instructed? Up to a point: very small children will, more or less, accept the dogma of their role models. In fact, it could be said that this is precisely what they're built to do at that point; to observe the world, absorb its input, and make sense of it. Paradigms, moral landmarks and reference points are easily assimilated in the early years: just ask the Hitler Youth.[7] Just speak to any four-year-old white who says that Asians are 'dirty', the Westboro Baptist child who celebrates the death of homosexual soldiers, the nursery preacher who tells his peers that they're going to Hell. Monkey see, monkey – depressingly often enough – do. But there are two very important caveats here: one is that the influence of family and peer groups is overwhelmingly more powerful than a few homilies and platitudes, however repetitively they are reinforced at school. The second is that by the time the child has entered even nursery school much of the job has been done: character has taken embryonic form, and home attitudes have been absorbed. The teacher is a late arrival to the party, and in the game of cognitive formation, the early bird catches the worm.

As the child grows up, character calcifies and reinforces itself; the best meant course of moral instruction finds itself increasingly deflected by pre-existing values and mores. What they are told starts to become filtered through the sieve of their prejudices and assimilated frames of reference. Tell a boy who believes that immigration *is* a big problem that it isn't, and see what he does with the information. Certainly, by the time that children reach secondary school, it would take a curriculum of enormous impact to shake established beliefs about ethics and culture.

This isn't to say that matters of cultural wisdom aren't to be communicated to children – this is part of their socialization process, and an unshakeable part of the process by which children receive their cultural heritage from adults. But any claim that such a process should be the aim of education trivializes the process by which it happens. Children learn values by observing how people act, not how they speak. The problem with assuming that teachers should be *formally* responsible for the moral progress of children is to place an unanswerable burden on the shoulders of a profession that has no formal process for doing so. It is beyond doubt that teachers should be *part* of this process, in an informal way; but this responsibility lies at the feet of *every* adult in the community, not simply teachers: parents, carers, and people in the street – *everyone* is responsible for looking after children.

Another problem is that the values to be imparted have themselves been decided and imposed 'from above'. This is a significant obstacle.

---

[7] I claim immunity from Godwin's Law at this point, for reasons of relevance.

It is one thing to say that schools should reinforce and demonstrate existing community values. It is entirely another matter to say that they must create new values, perhaps in community contexts where it is perceived that there is a lack: anti-racism, perhaps, or an appreciation for renewable energies. One obvious example of this would be the requirement for all schools in England and Wales to provide Citizenship education to all pupils, culminating for some in a formal GCSE at Key Stage 4. The explicit aim of this curricular bolt-on was to 'promote and encourage community cohesion, through a practical and experiential engagement with community representation.'

And this is why we have seen schools being increasingly seen as the panacea to the ills of society, whenever a problem is identified in the greater national community. It is easy for politicians to turn to schools as the Philosopher's Stone of social ills and say, 'If only we can nip (x) in the bud…' But this approach, while perhaps understandably seductive to anyone who wants to effect social change, deliberately ignores the other sectors of public life that actually demonstrate the social evil under scrutiny.

For example: say you have a mass decline in electoral turnout in the post-18 community. It's possible to see this as a problem, not with young people, but with the way politicians conduct themselves, and something that should perhaps be better dealt with by improving the quality of civic life at a parliamentary level. The expenses scandal of 2010, for instance, provides one example of why many might see politics as a slimy game with which to engage.

But no: the solution, the 'fix' is often perceived to be most efficacious if tackled at the level of the nursery, the classroom. Children are to be encouraged to re-engage with politics and civil life by instruction in the classroom; by engaging in mock parliaments; by drawing up children's manifestos and forming school councils and teen, shadow mayors with plastic rattles instead of a mace. This is like attempting to clean up a toilet by training people to enjoy the smell of flatulence.

What is a teacher?

With this in mind, we can repeat the original question that brought us here. A teacher is a professional who educates. What do they educate children in? The legacy of civilizations that have come before, or, to reduce that to something less transcendental, the subject in which the teacher is a specialist. If you have a degree in maths, may I suggest you teach them the joys of Pythagoras, differential calculus and Venn diagrams? I would also suggest that you don't spend too much time imagining that it's your job to make them happy, or learn how to value self-esteem, except incidentally, not explicitly, through the content of your lessons.

Is that all? Of course not: as I mentioned, simply by being a responsible adult in charge of a group or groups of students you will be tacitly responsible for many other informal aspects of their education, such as the aims I have mentioned above: helping them to learn how to conduct themselves; to work hard; to delay gratification for greater gain elsewhere; to be civil and responsible....the list goes on and on. But this will only happen indirectly, and rarely in the way you intend. You will of course, want to attempt to train them into good habits, which will serve them well in the subject you teach and life in general: persistence, problem solving, concentration, etc. But this will come about through the subject you teach, not as an activity in itself. Try teaching someone to concentrate, without giving them an object to focus on. Not so easy.

The conclusion I have come to might not seem particularly groundbreaking, especially to the amateur observer – telling someone that an English teacher's primary, explicit role is to teach English might seem like the least surprising conclusion since the School of Hard Knocks released their paper 'Fire is Hot'. But this simple elegant conclusion has been shredded in the last one hundred years or so. The educational biosphere is bubbling with opinions, ideologues, bloggers and interest groups, who all perceive the purpose of education (and implicitly the role of teachers) as one of the many options I outlined above; who view the role of schools as a transformative one; that the evils of cruelty, prejudice, injustice and inequality can all be washed away in the healing glow of education; that human nature itself can be moulded to the cast of a better potter. *Give me a child,* the Jesuit proverb says, *and I will give you the man.* Try telling that to my Citizenship class.[8]

A teacher is a professional who educates. Now that we know what we're supposed to do, we can take another step: how do we best do that? To answer that question, we have to investigate what must surely seem like the Philosopher's Stone of this discussion. How are state school teachers expected by the government to teach?

---

[8] I'd happily give some of my kids to a Jesuit, just to see what happens. That would teach him.

Teaching is a racket

Nobody – and I mean nobody – has a monopoly on the truth in education. Don't let anyone else tell you otherwise; even me. There will always be whores in this business who want to rob the pennies from your eyes and sell them back to you at interest. The teaching game has become a racket; everyone has an axe to grind and a theory. It is vital that you are aware of this as a teacher today: that it is a field composed of opinion and subjective truth, wrapped up and presented to you as fact.

But you wouldn't know it from the experience of being a teacher in the contemporary classroom. If you train as a teacher in the UK in the early decades of the twenty-first century you could be excused for thinking that Moses had descended from Mount Ararat with not two austere tablets of minimalist ethical wisdom, but a frosted folder of ring-bound, triple-punched closely-typed notes corresponding to every practical and theoretical situation that a teacher's career could ever encompass, with best practice and recommended reading punctuating the margins in italic desperation.

Every teacher is now burdened with the invisible albatross of a skyscraper of assumptions about what does and doesn't constitute good teaching. The other shoulder is balanced with equally Leviathan catechisms about what constitutes good learning. Let's examine the evidence, and in the manner of good social scientists, make up some reasons why we're right:

What constitutes good teaching?

It's easy to know what good teaching means. You might have thought that this was a complicated, subtle debate, animated for centuries by the practical and conceptual wisdom of the millions of practitioners. You would be very, very wrong. It's not hard at all: you can read it in about three pages. In fact you can even Google it, that's how easy it is.[9] Where is this Fountain of Wisdom? Ofsted, of course, the hired muscle of the DfE; formerly Her Majesty's Inspectors, until everyone realized how elegantly threatening it sounded, and it was replaced with the usual standardized, bastardization of common English

---

[9] Although apparently even that effort is beyond the majority of sixth formers, unless you ask them to investigate *The Da Vinci Code* or why the moon landing was faked.

that is de rigueur in the bureaucratic sphere; Ofsted, with its surly deliberate nod to Newspeak, *mini-ed* and *doubleplussatisfactory*, the unlovely, unloved protection racket of education. They, apparently, have all the answers.

Here's the story; I'm sure you're familiar with this. Schools aren't actually told how to teach by the government – that would be intrusive and micromanaging, of course. Schools are required to provide many things – a safe environment, a certain core curriculum, warm radiators and light bulbs, a venue for the silent tears of generations – but they are free from coercion in the sphere of teaching.

Except that they're not. Because once every three or four years along come the Inspectors[10] who proceed to eyeball everything that can be eyeballed; these things are judged and graded. Now the gradings are very important; if you get a 4 (or unsatisfactory, which is how the language of the machine works) then expect shame and penury to follow you; if the school earns a 4 overall, it enters Special Measures, which is another shorthand term for being turned into glue. Getting a notice of Special Measures is like the Department of Health putting a big sign on your restaurant door saying '*The food here is made from rotting wasps. If you eat it you will die.*'

So although the whole idea of freedom in the classroom has nominally been retained, this is not the reality. We all know that if we don't teach the way that Ofsted are looking for then they'll clobber us with their tedious certainties. So everyone dances around like giddy debutantes, trying to catch their eye with the latest fashionable educational ideas, making sure that we've stuffed ourselves into corporate corsets and rubbed lipstick over our faces to cover the cracks in our smiles and the tears running down our faces.

There is a painful orthodoxy within the teaching profession, where it is assumed that there are some features that characterize good teaching, and in their absence we should consider the teaching to be deficient. If I can direct us back to my original statement of intention...

A teacher is a professional who educates.
...then we can question this orthodoxy: educating is the key. Whatever method works towards that aim is an effective one; whatever doesn't, is not. It is similar to the way in which we see good

---

[10] Yes, they are still called inspectors, although I imagine that eventually they'll be referred to as change facilitators or something, and then Satan will rule the earth properly. Hail Azazel!

and bad behaviour. In my work as a behaviour adviser, I am often asked to define bad behaviour. My answer is simple: bad behaviour is anything that impedes the pupils' learning. That wonderful piece of conceptual rhetoric enables me to reward and sanction as I, the teacher, see fit, based on whether or not the pupil is acting in such a way to assist or deter my purpose. Of course, such a system entails that I be the teacher; that I hold the educational welfare as being paramount; that I don't tie myself in knots worrying if the kids are all loving it, or are at various points along the spectrum of inspiration. Are they being educated? Am I being the teacher? That's all I need to know; it's all they need me to be.

Why is this important?

This IS important, because the contemporary teacher is now being asked to assume so many burdens of objective that it is easy for the practitioner to become swamped. Later on, in Chapter 3, I'll explore how the teaching profession has reached this point, and the historical and political influences that have brought us here. As a teacher, you will be asked to perform duties that range from the academic to the pastoral; you might be tasked with making sure children are happy; inspired; emotionally literate; burning with self-esteem, among other intangibles. This mission creep is an extremely new phenomenon; to the new recruit into the profession, it might feel like the world has always been like this.

It has not. But even if the landscape of teaching doesn't change for a thousand years (and rest assured, change is the one invariable variable. You could bet your last kidney on it) then the teacher needs to be certain of this premise: these things are not part of being a teacher. You might be asked to do them; you might even be legally required to do them, but they are not teaching; they are not part of your role as a teacher. If society demands that we also assume the mantle of spectacularly bad pop psychologists, parents and social workers, then so be it. But we need to keep clear in our minds what we are as teachers, and that's what my focus is in this book. I can live with being a lousy inspirational figure, although I hope I can inspire; I can sleep at night if my students don't have radioactively positive self-esteem. But I cannot be a poor teacher and look at myself in the mirror.

Society may ask us to be a hundred things. In the same way that you can go to a locksmith and find that he also offers a shoe-repair service, roles can become entangled in an odd, historical sense. But a cobbler is not a locksmith.[11] And neither are we.

Educational research

Education has no aims. This may appear controversial, but a brief linguistic analysis reveals it to be a necessary truth. Education has no aims; *people* have aims. So the question 'what are the aims of education?' is transformed to 'who are the educators, and what have their aims been?'

It is important to involve a historical discussion in the pursuit of this question for several reasons: primarily, because teaching is such an ancient profession, one might expect that teachers themselves might have played an active and militant role in its inception, evolution and execution. Given the longevity and international context of the profession, it would also be reasonable for an uninformed observer to assume that the profession has benefited from an incremental and progressive improvement as centuries have passed; that the empirical understanding of one generation's teachers were promptly passed on to the next generation, where it was assessed, reviewed, dissected and absorbed into future understanding and subsequent dissemination to successors.

This may have been the case had education followed the paradigm of chemistry or other physical sciences such as engineering or architecture and civil engineering. These disciplines are, loosely speaking, empirically based; principles can be tested against known controls; measures of probability can be assessed, discussed, discarded or adopted. Of course the epistemological assessment of physical science is far more complex than this: there are numerous questions of how sciences categorize, relate to each other and assess causality, to name but a few of the very live topics of epistemological debate in natural philosophy; but taking an independent, material world external to us, consistent in its essence and powers as a given, it is possible to draw a broad line of progress, or at least depict it diagrammatically, however three-dimensional and complex the picture needs to be. Of course, this model does not take into account periods of historical forgetfulness, regression, misadventure and loss, where progress was anything but guaranteed or linear.

---

[11] How ON EARTH did that happen?

This is a simple model, but a useful one, offering an equally simple but useful contrast to the model of education. In this field, progress is much harder to quantify. What the aims are seems to vary from generation to generation, although perhaps always within a broad spectrum of aims. What we *should* teach children, also seems constrained by matters of value rather than matters of fact, and propels us to the conclusion that perhaps these aspects of education are similar to philosophical discussions of whether moral progress is possible, and whether ethics can be a cognitive pursuit, generating facts open to dispute and analysis, but ultimately given to resolution and agreement by rational minds. That analysis belongs to a whole other book.

Perhaps the third question – how do we best *teach* children? – is the one most susceptible to empirical observation and agreement. If, for instance, we can accept that the human individual is an example of a species with a biological taxonomy representative of its kind, then we might be able to infer common psychological or neurological behaviours that might then be susceptible to evaluation and classification. Therefore it might be reasonable to assume that certain teaching processes have greater impact or efficiency than others, and that some methods would have clear advantages over other methods; that by a Darwinian process of survival, these teaching memes might be influenced by environmental pressure and experience selection based on utility. The strong ideas would thrive, and weak teaching methods would wither on the vine.

If this is the case, then the major competitions to survive occurred at the very earliest peripheries of recorded human civilization. At the Agoras, Socrates would deliver lectures to students; later his grand student Aristotle would do the same, teaching by lecture and by setting his students guided research tasks from which they would then return and discuss. From this arbitrary starting point we can briskly follow the history of teaching methods, taking a broad view of its characteristics, until we fast forward to the late twentieth-century to come to at least one conclusion: broadly speaking at least, the method of instruction has changed extremely little. The paradigm of the instructor, an educated, experienced guide, imparting knowledge and skills to less experienced students using a relatively small range of methods – lecturing, discussion, independent work, but primarily reading, writing and speaking – reached its evolutionary point at an extremely distant point in the past. Descartes tutored Queen Christina of Sweden in a very similar way to any individually educated pupil;[12] John Stuart Mill's unusual home schooling[13] experience, while seemingly crushingly restrictive, shares its DNA with the 1980s US vogue for hothousing more than it does with anything else. It has been noted that, were one magically to transplant a teacher from the fifth century BC into a twentieth-century classroom,[14] then that teacher would have a fundamental and intuitive understanding of the processes taking place in both institutions.

The same could not be said of a technician in just about any field of the natural sciences: if Hippocrates were to be set loose in the cardiac theatre of St Thomas' emergency ward in Westminster, he would probably slay more patients than he saved. A mason from thirteenth-century Genoa would be more mystified by the gravity-defying reinforced concrete of London's South Bank than anything else. Teaching processes have resisted intrinsic or structural redesign for a very long time. This is not to assume that there are no improvements to be made in the field, or that further research is invalid; merely to suggest that such a long-lived paradigm in such a variety of eras and civilizations suggests a near-optimal suitability that can be tentatively compared to the longevity of the shark, crocodile or cockroach in nature. It could be said that the methodology of teaching occupies a state of evolutionary equilibrium.

Of course the immediate response to this claim could perhaps be to say that this is a reactionary position; that it is a conservative appeal to the wisdom of the ancients that defies and denies the necessity and efficacy of progress. Such an attitude, its detractors might say, would have crushed innovation in its crib and denied successive generations the benefits of the fruits of innovation, enterprise and risk. Fine. There is no argument against this, because no such argument could ever be won: innovation is beneficial. So too is recognizing the value of hard-earned lessons learned. This is not, cannot, be a debate between the relative merits of change versus stability, any more than one could have an intelligent debate about whether fast was better than slow. Suffice it to say that we change the traditional model of

---

[12] Funny story about Descartes: when he was ten, a physician advised him never to get up early or he would DIE (every child's fantasy diagnosis). Later on, at the behest of the notorious early-rising Queen he was tutoring, he was forced to do so. He was dead in *six months*. FACT.

[13] I say 'unusual': the poor chap could read Herodotus in the original Greek by the age of eight. He had a mental breakdown by the age of 18. He also thought his upbringing was 'unremarkable'. These days, you'd have the social services round like the SAS.

[14] Perhaps there's a skills shortage.

teaching with care, not the lunatic, breathtaking speed of most people who advocate classroom revolutions. Have you noticed how they usually have something they want to sell? Just saying.

Another theory of good teaching: Wittgenstein's Theory of Familial Resemblance

Establishing exactly what we mean by excellent teaching is slippery beyond belief; whenever you try to define it, you fall into traps of abstract, infinite regression. There are core standards accredited by teaching ministries, which all focus on tangibles, things that can be measured, compared and assessed. And who can blame such an approach? Many may bemoan the situation where school inspection and lesson observations rely on such blunt, dull data as grades and target value-added figures, but if I were the governor in charge of a billion-dollar budget (I'm not, but open to offers) then I probably wouldn't just drop a bag of swag on the desk of the teaching bodies and say, 'See what you can do with all that. No, no, just do your best.' It's entirely understandable that such a huge public contribution should require some kind of monitoring and, dare I say it, assessment.

But every time you try to describe great teaching, while there may be some constants, it very quickly becomes obvious that there are an enormous number of teachers we would consider great, but they all possess qualities that may be very, very different. There are Nordic robots and earth mothers, messianic enthusiasts and paper pushers. They can all be transformative teachers. How do we square this inconsistency? How can we say what a great teacher is if we cannot establish a set of definitive characteristics that allow us to develop a taxonomy of pedagogic best practice?

The answer lies in a different direction: instead of trying to catch the phantom of great teaching and putting it under a microscope, we should embrace the fact that it lies more seriously in the realm of the abstract than the concrete; to try to define it is to try to grasp a fairy tale with a steel claw. They exist in different planes.

Take the devilishly simple question: what is art? Philosophers have tried to create a meaningful definition as long as men have painted bears on cave walls. You try it. Not so easy. So many things, you see, appear to be art, but they have so little in common: paintings, of course, and sculpture. And ballet, and dance, and opera, and dirty hip-hop, and the bricks in the Tate, and John Cage's 4'33'', and

Hirst's *The Physical Impossibility of Death in the Mind of the Living*, and so on and so on. What do they have in common?

Another example is 'games'. What is a game? Football, yes; and tennis; and Scrabble, and Cluedo, and solitaire, and chess, and wall ping-pong, and so on and so on. What does solitaire have to do with competitive high-board diving? What is a game? It's a slippery fish to grasp.

Wittgenstein famously answered this: he described all such activities as members of a set, some of which overlapped with each other, and some of which did not. He called it *Family Resemblance*. Football is like Snap![15] in that it is competitive; and Snap! is like solitaire in that they are both played with cards. In this way, we can find resemblances between members of a set, but not necessarily between all of them, or sometimes even anything that they all share.

This applies to teaching, and great teachers too. They can be as different as golf and gammon steaks, but they share one thing in common: kids learn with them. Everything else is chaff, and we need to start to wake up to the fact that there is no perfect paradigm of the perfect teacher. The teacher that flourishes in the ghettoes of inner-city warzone classrooms might sink in the private sector of well-supported angels – different skill sets, different contexts, different levels of virtue needed. There is no one ideal teacher, just as there isn't an ideal dinner, an ideal day, or a perfect comeback. It all depends on context; it all depends on the teacher, the subject, the student, the classroom, the weather, solar flare activity and a million other things.

Now we have established what a teacher really is, we're now going to have a history lesson. It's a very special history lesson, because it's the history of you, or at least the history of education in the UK, and a little beyond, and by extension the history of the teacher. Many teachers arrive at their first jobs seemingly under the impression that the role was invented five minutes prior to their contract. It may surprise you to know that there have been teachers for thousands of years, as long as there has been a cultural and intellectual legacy to impart and inherit.

Marx believed that before the workers of the world would unite and throw off their chains, they first had to acknowledge that they were workers, and that they were in chains. I invite you now to understand that you are a teacher, in a continuum of teachers. I leave

---

[15] Exclamation mark compulsory.

it to you to ascertain if the chains around your ankles are leg-irons or daisies.

This is your history.

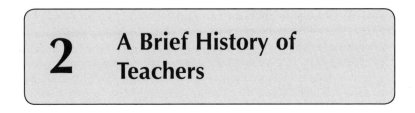

2 A Brief History of Teachers

'AH ... SUCH AS THE ANCIENTS POSSESSED.'

Where did you come from? Teachers haven't sprung ex nihilo from the womb of modernity. The teacher is as ubiquitous a character in human history as the beggar and the doxy, for as long as there was any teaching to be done. The history of education is the history of the teacher. In this chapter I'll explore the growth of education and the teacher in the UK – and beyond, in case there are any teachers in Tonga reading this and feeling left out.[1]

The first teachers we would recognise in Britain were Roman. Of course they were. At the same time as they were building viaducts and under-floor central heating, refining Noric steel and inventing humiliation entertainment, we were probably just about finding out that you couldn't breathe pebbles. Private tutors would accompany the immigrant convoys to keep the children of aristocrats educated.

---

[1] In which case, Ha'u 'o Va'inga: 'Omai e pa'anga 'e tolu nima.

Once they had become fed up of with our drizzly weather and taste for sarcasm, and wisely withdrawn to the fabulous Shangri-la of the Mediterranean so that they could collapse the Empire properly, education in Britain reverted back to its prior, swampy form.

In pre-literate societies, the most common educational paradigm was to learn everything from your parents; class systems were reinforced until they became caste systems, not by choice but through necessity; the labour of your father was your labour, and your trade. Social norms, community values, hygiene, survival skills and industry were all learned in the same place, with the added attraction of being oral in nature. In many societies, Britain included, memorization was a vital skill to master, which is a bit of a shock to modern enemies of times tables.

As societies expanded, labour began the inevitable specialization of division; trades developed, as people naturally differentiated their crafts into specialisms, which massively improved productivity by virtue of efficiency. Carpentry; masonry; artisans, smiths, farmers could all exist in social contract with one another, to the mutual benefit of the group. The most common educational paradigm at this point was still the apprenticeship, although now it could be performed at the knee of local experts and masters rather than simply and inevitably by the family. Anything other than these basic skills were the province of the very wealthy or the career priest. Literacy, at one point as exciting and revolutionary an invention as the computer or light bulb, was still the exclusive privilege of the few: those involved in government, the Church or trade, where the ability to keep records and communicate precisely remained necessary – money and religion: two eternal motivators. No doubt you find this hard to believe in our contemporary societies, where the love of money is non-existent, and religion has all but withered on the vine.

No schools existed, not in the sense we would recognize. Then, the only place where young people would gather to learn from an instructor would be in the monasteries, after their parents had entered them (sometimes from the age of seven) to the apprenticeship of priesthood. I like to imagine that even then children would still ask, 'Why are we studying religion anyway?'[2] The only qualification needed to teach – and this, as we'll see, is a common theme – was that the teacher was an expert in the topic being taught. Pedagogic ability wasn't a consideration.

---

[2] Only back then, I imagine that they could be beaten with a shitty chain just for asking.

Returning to the growth of the UK education system, we see a slow process that eventually led to civil education, at first restricted to the children of privilege or of the monasteries, coupled with home education and apprenticeships, gradually expanding to include larger and larger segments of the common population, until education moved from a privilege to a right to a requirement. This transition was inspired, as we shall see, by a complex matrix of social and economic triggers, largely extrinsic to the classroom. Pragmatism, survival and necessity were the inspiration for these processes, not the concerns of a government, sensitivity to the modern concept of a national (or international) economy, or the motors of ideology. Teachers were certainly the last instrument of the process, coming once again at the end of long chain of functional necessity. There was no prescriptive system beyond practicality.

Transmitting skills from one generation to the next was conducted on a basis of local utility, balanced with the availability of experienced craftsmen, scholars and artisans. Of course, in high status families, home schooling was an option, unavailable to most, where children could be instructed in skills and fields not intrinsically linked to generating an income – at least not directly. Philosophy, theology, etiquette, falconry, were all as possible to pursue for the son of a wealthy landowner or feudal lord as animal husbandry and farming. But these less utilitarian skills were required shibboleths, and can be seen, indirectly, as conferring a social survival advantage over the less educated.

Grammar schools started to appear in the early sixth-century, usually as annexes to monasteries and abbeys. The instruction was focused on Latin, music, mathematics and law. The reasoning behind this curriculum was pragmatic and religious: the students were training for the priesthood, and those subjects were essentially vocational. The grammar schools became part of a preparation for higher study at this time, providing the Trivium[3] to the classical education system. In the twelfth-century the first ancient Universities were founded, Oxford and Cambridge,[4] and in the fourteenth- and

---

[3] The Trivium was the medieval undergraduate degree, composed of logic, grammar and rhetoric, which preceded the harder quadrivium (hence *Trivial*, because it was comparatively easier, which should tell you something about the centuries-old heritage of dumbing-down).

[4] Five minutes after which they were both accused of elitism and creating a two-tier education system, until they pointed out that state education wouldn't be invented for several hundred years.

fifteenth-centuries the first schools independent of the churches – Winchester and then Eton – were founded. Once again, the role of the teacher was defined by forces beyond his control. The teaching method was understood to be an intuitive process that did not require complication or experimentation.In fact, part of the Trivium – rhetoric – explicitly involved the method of persuasion and instruction; this showed that teaching was largely a matter of expertise and the ability to ask sound, leading questions.[5]

In 1563 The Statute of Artificers and Apprentices required all apprenticeships to be seven years, ensuring some kind of rigour in vocational training, and simultaneously consolidating the political control of the guilds over careers in the trades and crafts. The Poor Law of 1691 provided for the children of paupers to become apprentices. During the Industrial Revolution it was decided that 'new' industries were exempt from the Statute of Apprenticeships, opening the door to an even more diffuse system of training for the opportunities afforded by industrialization.[6]

The Sunday School movement of the mid-eighteenth-century started to provide for the education of the 'wretched' poor, taking place on a Sunday in order not to disrupt working in factories for the other six days of the week. This was initiated by Robert Raikes, a publisher, who believed that the set text for the boys should be the Bible; the lessons were reading and catechisms. Already we see an embryonic system of schooling, with aims, method (mainly repetition and recital) and a curriculum. The teacher's presence is still only felt in the classroom; those with the means to create schools also enjoyed the privilege of defining practice, method and content. But this wasn't an age of experimentation and frivolity; schools were tools to produce children who would inherit the legacy of the past, and maintain the fabric of existent societies.

This process of expanding the franchise proceeded as the centuries progressed – provision was enabled by Royal decree (for example, the Royal Schools of Ulster instituted by James I) or by enlightened philanthropists or by the Church. But it must be remembered that throughout this period the vast majority of children never saw the inside of a classroom; their labour was too valuable to their families to waste in education. But in the sixteenth to the eighteenth centuries it became popular for wealthy noblemen or guilds to create grammar schools, especially after the Reformation.

---

[5] Something that speaks volumes to me across the centuries.
[6] Read: 'exploited'.

By the mid-eighteenth-century, a growing commercial class created a demand for an education system that taught more than the conjugation of verbs or parsing. But many grammar schools, restricted by the terms of their original foundations, were unable to teach anything other than those subjects specified by the terms, usually Latin or Greek. In 1805 the Lord Chancellor, Lord Eldon, reluctantly ruled that there was no legal means to justify rescinding the terms of those foundations, and the type of schools that they provided for. He allowed an iota of compromise by admitting some schools could teach, for example, French *in addition* to the set curriculum, but this was a token admission at best. At this stage, teachers were not only a silent voice in the process of a still static curriculum, but we can see that they provided far less of a voice than commercial interests who were pressing for change.

Still, up to this point in history, if the teacher was *persona non gratis* as far as deciding school policy, it could conversely be seen as a Golden Age for their status as a professional. After all, they may not have been able to provide any input worth mentioning into the curriculum; they may have had ideological and pedagogical restrictions, but they were relatively free from inspection; they were judged by the success of their students; and they relied on the quality of their reputations. Free from the tribulations of policy churn that the modern professional contends with, they at least had the ability to teach as they pleased, albeit within prescribed parameters.

This persisted until the Grammar Schools Act of 1840, which allowed grammar schools to use fees to fund pursuits other than Latin and Greek; the 1869 Endowed Schools Act provided the legal mechanism for grammar schools finally to restructure their offer to include science, languages and commercial subjects. Again, the pressure for reform came not specifically from teachers, but was generated by extrinsic factors such as public and parental pressure, expressed as legal reform.

Education was still a private affair for the vast majority – wealthy parents voluntarily referred their children to fee-paying schools. William Edward Forster's Elementary Education Act of 1870 made provision compulsory for all children between the ages of five and thirteen. Compulsory *provision*, but not compulsory attendance; local school boards could be set up to enforce attendance, with farm labourers allowed to leave early to return to work in the fields. There were many exemptions even from these boards – for example, if children were ill, or lived a certain distance from the nearest school. Most interestingly, children were allowed to leave school once they had reached a predetermined level of academic achievement, rather than being forced to attend until a set chronological age; something that has been reversed in the modern British system, where children advance though the curriculum irrespective of achievement.

Still, widespread attendance did not become mandatory until the 1880 Elementary Education Act, with all children aged five to ten affected. Interestingly, it was not until 1893 that this requirement was binding on blind or deaf children, heralding the introduction of Special Needs education. In 1891 the Free Education Act created an embryonic school voucher system, with the state paying up to ten shillings a week for each child. Lord Balfour's Education Act of 1902 replaced school boards with Local Education Authorities, and meant that all schools, grammar or state, could be funded through taxes. This makes a mockery of the widely held belief that our educational system has an ancient heritage; in every practical sense, it is less than a hundred years old.

After World War One, the Fisher Act made attendance compulsory up until the age of fourteen, and secondary schools (which had been recognised in 1900) were largely subject to the state. Many grammar schools sought to switch status and be governed by their LEA. Although the Fisher Act also provided for compulsory state education for those between the ages of fourteen and eighteen, this radical reform was shelved by the arrival of the Second World War.

The invention of the modern education system

This progressive programme of enabling access via public institutions began to centralize and institutionalize the aims and structures of education. Up until this point in history, it had rarely been questioned that the aims of education were to be different for different children; some were to be taught a trade, some would be trained in Latin to recite catechisms, and others would not be trained at all, there being no perceived need that an apprenticeship couldn't meet. To the modern mind, this seems counter-intuitive; one of the unifying themes of modern education has been justice, equality and fairness. Of course, these concepts are relative – fair to whom? Equal in what respect? Opportunity, outcome or provision? – but there has been some consensus at a national level that all students (of a certain age) should not only be educated, but also have an entitlement to such education; that entitlement has become a requirement, is blind to income, gender, ethnicity or ability. Berlin And Fromme would describe this as positive liberty; by restricting children in one way, we free them in another; in this case, requiring them to attend school, in order that their lives may be forced to be free from the chains of poverty and ignorance.

What drove this expansion of suffrage? Pragmatism, certainly. Hundreds of thousands of unoccupied children entailed a restriction on the adult workforce, and presented enormous challenges to the security of a community – the 'keep them off the streets' argument. Connected to this is the need to mobilize a large workforce, who presumably had to learn their skills somewhere – too important a responsibility to leave to chance. The growth in civil rights that accompanied the Trade Union and Labour movements undoubtedly had an impact on this process too; we could look also to Liberals like John Stuart Mill, who argued for an increase in suffrage and economic provision for the lower classes as a moral imperative and also as a way to maximize social happiness.

Other philosophical and political movements, following the Enlightenment with its emphasis on the importance of man, the nobility of human nature and the concept of Universal Rights, undoubtedly assisted this process through society. The Industrial Revolution created the need to train an enormous urban working class. And the teacher was the passive recipient of these grand ideas, the proletariat to the vast rolling forces of economic pressures and the means of production, to give it a Marxist perspective.

The 1944 Education Act continued the top-down approach to educational reform. The tripartite system of schooling was introduced to society – the Grammar School, the Technical School, and the Secondary Modern. At least one of the explicit aims of this reform was to generate a tailored workforce to meet what was considered to be the needs of society – leaders, skilled labourers and everyone else. In many ways it reflected Plato's Republican ideal, with its men of Gold, Silver and Bronze. Note that this reform was again driven by economic considerations: not by reflection or feedback from the army of teachers;[7] not by pressure placed on the system by the still relatively disorganized unions. Teachers were expected to deliver the content in the same way a postman was expected to deliver the mail. (Significantly, the 1944 Act was intended to be introduced in 1939, but it was decided not to overburden the war economy. And even so, it wasn't until 1947 that it was implemented.)

---

[7] Not an army, I'd like to say, that I'd be happy sending against anything more sinister than an invasion of jelly babies.

Still, in contrast to this perspective, we can also see the 1944 Act as ushering in a silver age of teacher power – although the structural formation of the tripartite reform was enacted despite high levels of concern from teachers and the educational establishment. Head teachers had an enormous level of influence on school curriculum content, in agreement with governing bodies. Although this devolution of power was still not directly linked to the classroom practitioner, it had come extremely close; and most head teachers had obtained office via teaching, which brought large levels of empirical experience to their decisions. The Schools Council was formed, which enjoyed high levels of input from teachers on a consultative basis, although it was still a state institution.

It is worth noting that the Act said very little about the curriculum (other than religious education) and its authors clearly did not anticipate national government interfering in the curriculum. It was left to the teaching profession to decide what to teach and how to teach it. In fact the minister did not have the legal right to determine the content of education and, in the phrase first used by Conservative Minister of Education Sir David Eccles in 1960, was not expected to enter 'the secret garden of the curriculum'.[8]

The tripartite system was exposed to claims of elitism and explicit social engineering, and eventually the Comprehensives were introduced; open to all, with no entrance exams, like Holland Park School in West London. The leaving age crept up to 16 in 1973.

The teaching profession by this time enjoyed a large amount of influence; particularly in Higher Education, there was a 'gentlemen's agreement' that matters of education were best dealt with, administered and discussed by those in the profession – the 'secret garden' into which ministers were only invited to hear the results of discussions from within, and into which the public – families, students, interested third parties – were not invited at all. Stakeholders were still decades away. The Schools Council had been created; the unions had grown in power since their inception at the turn of the century; they had even managed to streamline themselves into a handful of bodies which meant that they could command large numbers of teacher professionals as members, and therefore enjoy influence in decision-making.

In 1976, the PM James Callaghan launched the 'Great Debate' at Ruskin College, Oxford, explicitly warning the educational

---

[8] Gillard, D. (2007) *Education in England: a brief history* www.educationengland.org.uk/history

establishment that they should expect to become more open to outside influence if they expected to enjoy continued public funding. This speech marked a growing involvement of government in curriculum decision-making, a process that would eventually see a more perfect evolution in the Conservative governments of the coming years. Still, even though government influenced education through HMIs and involvement in the Schools Council, 'the nearer one comes to the professional content of education, the more indirect the Minister's influence is' (Kogan 1971: 172).

Then, in 1979, the bombshell of Thatcherism rocked the education profession in an unprecedented way. Although any new political movement can be explained as a product of its environment (rising unemployment, general dissatisfaction with the left-wing governance of the incumbent Labour administration, and a thousand other matters of public discontent), it is generally agreed that Mrs Thatcher's personal impact on educational policy thereafter was considerable. National Vocational Qualifications, the Assisted Places scheme and the Youth Training Scheme followed. But the Education Reform Act of 1988 was for once an aptly described bill, enacting a stream of policy changes that affected education in the UK at a fundamental level.

Education moved into a market paradigm. Schools were expected to deliver a service to the students and their families, who could now be classed as consumers – or perhaps customers.[9] This quantum leap in ideology meant that unpopular (unsuccessful or possibly just unliked) schools would close, and successful schools would thrive. It was a Darwinian model that closely mirrored the belief that market forces were the most efficient and reliable mechanisms of delivering education. The National Curriculum was a result of the 1988 Act; with it came National Curriculum Assessments – SATs, League Tables and Formula Funding. Grant Maintained School status also allowed schools to opt out of LEA control, which foreshadowed the later Academies and Free Schools movement. These enormous new policy enactments meant an entirely new climate for teachers to work in and to adjust to.

'Conservative legislation sought to drive neo-liberal principles into the heart of public policy. An emphasis on cost reduction, privatization and deregulation was accompanied by vigorous measures against the institutional bases of Conservatism's opponents, and the

---

[9] If that conceptual legerdemain doesn't make your gorge rise, then I suggest that you are dead inside.

promotion of new forms of public management. The outcome of these processes was a form of governance in which market principles were advanced at the same time as central authority was strengthened.'[10]

Ironically, the Secretary of State for Education at this time, Sir Keith Joseph, was a staunch advocate of the independence and autonomy of schools; but despite this ideological disquiet, he oversaw the conceptual neo-liberal radicalization of modern education.

It must be said that teachers were far from silent at this stage. By the 1980s they had collectivized fairly effectively in several well-organized unions, who campaigned vociferously for wage increases and other workload issues; Thatcherite reforms inevitably meant job losses due to restructuring, an increased workload, and an ideological assumption of a monetarist model for education that many teachers in the largely left-wing unions found anathema to their beliefs about the aims and means of education. National strike action followed, the biggest the teaching profession had ever seen. A series of rolling strikes took place that went on for two years, prompting the creation of a special Cabinet Committee to deal with the issue. Unfortunately, the strike persisted so long, and interfered with so many families, that teachers lost a huge amount of sympathy in the public's eye – and seriously damaged the power of the unions, who were 'spent and exhausted' by the end of the strike action. After that point, unions and teachers would have far less influence in the way policy was enacted. In the words of Mike Baker, they were 'shunned' by successive governments, where previously they had enjoyed a collective influence.[11]

The Schools Council was abolished in 1984, and with it one of the last links between policy command centre and the teaching profession. Local Government, an obstacle to Thatcher's centralist reforms, was weakened in a succession of strategies: funding was cut to LEAs, and simultaneously their responsibilities were reduced. Media sympathetic to the Conservative mission fed the flames of public dissatisfaction towards LEA autonomy by misrepresenting their excesses – the 'Baa Baa White Sheep' scare-scandals that dominated the headlines for some time in the eighties were without foundation. Still, they served their purpose, and public sympathy drained from LEAs, or the 'loony left' by which they were increasingly portrayed as having been infiltrated.

---

[10] Jones 2003: 107
[11] news.bbc.co.uk/1/hi/education/7367471.stm

The Empire strikes back

At the same time, parental power was actively encouraged: parents on school governing bodies; parents making choices about which schools to send their children to; parents finally being able to examine school exam results and league tables. Non-professionals were encouraged to have influence on how schools were running, and make judgements on them by choosing – or withholding – their children from them. Parents were invited to be more than passive recipients of the school 'product' – they became stakeholders. 1992 saw the formation of Ofsted[12], which in many teachers' eyes was seen as watchdog, judge and jury for schools under the increasingly centralized control of the Department of Education. Deeply unpopular in the profession, its reports wielded considerable influence over a school's curriculum, methodology and process, given its public reports and ability to cast apparently authoritative judgements over schools and their practices. This, in conjunction with parental choice and examination league tables, has made it far more intrusive than its previous incarnation, HMI.

The 'New' Labour Government in 1997, rather than sweeping the education table and turning back the clock on the Thatcherite reforms, surprisingly (to some) carried on with many of the reforms of the previous two decades, committing to the market paradigm and continuing to deepen parental involvement, central planning and expansion of school choice. League tables and the National Curriculum survived the transition of power, and teachers who had believed that some of their disenfranchisement might be addressed with the return of a Labour government were sorely disappointed.

Through the Number Ten Policy Unit and significant advisors such as Lord Adonis, educational control was firmly placed in the direct control of the First Minister. Indeed, it was this centralization of power that allegedly led to the resignation of the then Education secretary, Estelle Morris. She and her successors were increasingly viewed as simply enacting policy that originated from Number Ten. Charles Clarke and Ruth Kelly were also widely viewed as having clashed with Blair and Adonis (unsuccessfully) over their limited leadership roles within the Education Department.

More national guidelines for a range of policies were created: numeracy and literacy strategies; gifted and talented provision; SEN

---

[12] Modelled on the Spanish Inquisition: only the guilty have anything to fear, and no one expects them.

provision; National Curriculum levels and concomitant targets. Some of these guidelines were requirements; some, like the non-statutory curriculum for Religious Education and other non-compulsory/ core subjects, were 'advised' suggestions.[13] Linking teacher pay progression to performance reviews, a policy that inspired the strikes of the eighties, was continued; selective grammar schools (what remained of them) were to be tolerated, unless 'parents wanted change'.[14] Centralization of education progressed even beyond the Thatcherite reforms; power seeped back not only to the Department of Education, but further, past even that and into the hands of the Prime Minister, who was undoubtedly aware of what every leader understands: reforming and controlling education is the easiest way to reform and recast society.

Stephen Byers embarked on a policy of 'naming and shaming schools' that were deemed to be failing by Ofsted, which inevitably contributed to their demise. The Excellence in Cities Initiative, designed to improve standards in inner-city environments by linking them with excellent ('beacon') schools, was run centrally from the Department of Education. Private consultants were sent into some failing schools and LEAs to advise on improvement strategies. If ever there was a symbol that not only the teaching profession, but the school system and the LEAs were being excluded from policy invention and execution, this was it. The age of the non-teaching, teacher 'expert' had arrived.[15]

Interestingly, at the same time as these policies excluded and marginalized teachers, the City Academy project was set up, which would allow schools to opt out partially of LEA control and enter private partnerships, which in turn would return some influence over curriculum and practice to the schools themselves. There was clearly a reforming tension within the New Labour project: on the one hand seemingly addicted to prescriptivism and micro-management; on the other advocating that some schools remove themselves from central government control almost completely. Specialist Schools, Private Public Partnerships and proposals in the 2001 White Paper to return 85 per cent of school budgets to the Head Teacher's control encouraged selective admission practices, a policy that had been anathema to Labour theorists only a decade before. Some saw

---

[13] In much the same way that the Triads 'advise' local businesses in China Town to 'invest' in protection.

[14] Blair, T.

[15] Greeted with the same level of enthusiasm as a turd in a Waldorf salad.

this project as hauntingly similar to the City Technology Colleges proposed by the Conservatives decades before. They certainly saw parallels with the City Academies project of much later, which was created by New Labour and continued – accelerated – under the Cameron/ Gove education administration.

The principle of selection and opting out was also boosted by offering funds to grammar schools in partnership schemes with comprehensives. Alasdair Campbell famously referred to comprehensives as 'bog-standard', a sentiment more poetically expressed by the Education Secretary Estelle Morris as 'one size fits all.' After a long period of centralization, with all the disenfranchisement issues for teachers that entailed, there was a strong movement within the Labour government to remove a segment of the school population from not only LEA control, but from central government control – although not funding. By 2004, teaching unions, revolted by selection and the Academy Schemes, demanded an abandonment of both policies. Central Government knew that it could ignore these calls; the Unions had by this point been reduced to just another pressure group. No industrial action ensued over those issues.

Towards the middle of the decade, an avalanche of protest began to accumulate against the excessive micro-management of schools, their policies and their curricula. The Chief Inspector David Bell warned that the National Curriculum focus on Maths, English and Science was leading to a 'two-tier' education system, at the expense of other subjects. He also noted that, despite the Labour government's insistence on inclusion – the habit of attempting to retain students, who would previously have been expelled, within mainstream education, and removing the Head's direct power to permanently exclude – only one in three schools exhibited an acceptable level of behaviour. Former Chief Inspector Mike Tomlinson warned that pupils were suffering from examination overload in the government's pursuit of target setting. Chris Woodhead, the first Chief Inspector, had long since resigned from Ofsted, citing New Labour's invasive and prescriptive interference in schools as his reason for leaving.

In 2004 the Tomlinson report made a number of wide ranging recommendations on 14–18 education, after extensive consultation with researchers and teaching bodies. It was essentially ignored by the government. The Every Child Matters initiative was inspired – some would say hastily – in response to the death of Victoria Climbie and the perceived failure of the social services in preventing her death. It is highly significant that an enormously influential piece of education policy (it required schools to make significant commitments to providing, amongst other things, 'enjoyment' and 'safety' in lessons)[16] resulted from a single instance of a child's death, and the context of that death. Again, this can be seen as exemplifying an environment where significant restructuring of education, with concomitant legislation passed in order to support it, completely bypasses the feedback of those who will be required to provide – in modern parlance 'deliver' – it.

The Dark Ages

This was a time of deepening distrust and resentment between teacher-professionals and the educational establishment, who late into their third term seemed to be digging in their heels in resistance to the wishes of the teaching community. It has been suggested that this is a consequence of long-term access to power, possibly because those in power imagine that they will always enjoy the entitlement that position accords them. Perhaps this was exemplified best by Tony Blair's decision to create a ministerial post for Lord Adonis, who had never held any ministerial post before, had not been elected, and was deeply unpopular with the teaching profession. Blair appointed him anyway.

It could even be argued that what representation is enjoyed by teachers through such bodies as unions, the Schools Council and the General Teaching Council (now abolished, to little mourning) is intrinsically unrepresentative anyway; the unions, although enjoying a large membership, are still segmented, and able to take action with only a small minority in agreement – in the 2008 one-day strikes over pay and conditions, industrial action was called on a 31 per cent turnout of 294,000 members, only 35 per cent of whom voted in favour of strike action. In other words, wide-scale school closures resulted from the affirmative consent of fewer than 40,000 teachers, set against an enormous majority that dissented, disagreed or simply didn't care. The GTC had long failed to unite teachers as a representative body, given its long status as the investigation, disciplinary and

---

[16] And thank God for that: previously on ER, we had been practising our crossbow skills using their heads as apple-stands, and trying to bore them to death. How stupid/ obvious does a policy have to be before someone won't try to encapsulate it in law? 'Oxygen must be freely available to all students.'

appeals body for teachers, rather than acting in any kind of advocacy role.[17]

This brief and broad analysis of the history of education in the UK naturally focuses on the late twentieth-century and the early twenty-first; still, it can be seen that the driving forces behind education have been, for the most part, inspired by economic, political and social forces beyond the control of teacher-professionals. The presumed expertise of the teaching profession is quickly marginalized, and apart from a significant period in the early-to late-twentieth-century when the teaching profession enjoyed a modicum of autonomy, is routinely subject to prescription, inspection and direction.

What about the rest of the world?

What about it? If you're reading this in the UK, you might be forgiven for asking if the experiences of the Lyceum or the Gymnasium have any relevance to you. On the other hand, educational experts, ministers, people who have access to the internet, all reliably pounce on the experiences of our foreign colleagues and forebears to justify their brainwaves. This is understandable: as I'll point out in Chapter 3, reliable educational research is hard to do and takes lots of people, lots of effort and funding. Why not just watch what the others are doing and take the best of their experiences? It works in the fields of technology; and schools are far from secretive about their methods. In fact, they're usually delighted to have us in their schools, showing off their latest progenies and smiling in a variously Slavic/Oriental, but invariably Scandinavian way. *See how we educate*, they say. *We are the masters of the world.*[18]

But how difficult it is simply to transfer results from one environment to another. It may very well be applicable for one country – let's call it Sweden – to have a system where children form school councils and make meaningful contributions to school affairs, organizing their own recycling festivals and meatball parties, and quite another to say that this ideal behaviour will be reproduced in, say, the special

---

[17] By the time it was put out of its misery, it seemed to exist solely to discipline errant teachers. Essential, but not really what you're looking for from your representative, is it?

[18] Which, presumably, is why Denmark and Finland are such economic global powerhouses. I'm kidding. They're gorgeous.

educational unit of Barlinnie Secondary school in Scotland. I suspect 'meatballs' would mean something else there.

A similar problem is encountered when we try to develop a national or international strategy for dealing with behaviour. On the one hand, we can say that some tactics will have a fairly reliable outcome: for example, punishing children tends to deter behaviour, and being prepared engenders more respect than being unprepared for lessons. But the problem of different cultures and contexts is that what works for one group may not work for another; there are too many other variables that muddy the analysis and defy the outcome. I have heard many behaviour 'experts' advise new recruits in tough schools, and tell them to organize games with them; do nothing but praise them; avoid detentions; get to know them by sharing personal information. That may well be a great way to deal with agreeable, mature, thoughtful students who simply need a bit of encouragement to get working. But it's career suicide in anything like an inner-city zoo, where the kids need to see that you're serious before they'll take you seriously. You can still do all the relationship-building high jinks, but the moment you forget that these kids need to see that you're in charge, they'll have you in a toastie.

Beware the behaviour wallahs.[19] Especially the ones that have never taught, or taught for about five minutes in a kind, warm village school in Dorset, and now preach to everyone else about how children just need to be understood, and wring their hands about how every bad behaviour is just the child trying to communicate something to you. Yes. They're communicating that they want a detention. See? Psychology's easy.

With that in mind, it's still useful to see how education evolved in what I'm going to refer to affectionately as 'the rest of the world', as I evidence as much sensitivity to national differences as your average *Streetfighter 2* game.

The Ancient Greeks and education

You can't avoid the Ancient Greeks in this debate. They predate and inspire Western civilization in a way that, despite the best efforts of twentieth-century educationalists, is undeniable. The Old Greece was broadly divided into two states: Athens and Sparta. The Spartan society was even more ridiculous, glorious and obsessive than

---

[19] Apart from me. I'm safe.

Hollywood would suggest. From birth to the age of seven, children were in the care of the mother – also trained as a warrior, and trained to raise her child as one. After that, the child would be trained by an older male to fight, until by the age of thirty they would be classed as warriors.[20]

The point of Spartan education was entirely geared to the sublimation of the individual to the state, the disintegration of the ego and its reorientation as an agent of Spartan civilization. Proponents of child-centred education would spit feathers, I imagine.[21] As Plutarch said, 'All the rest of their education was calculated to make them subject to command, to endure labour, to fight, and to conquer.' Put that in your pipe, Ofsted.[22]

Music, dance, religious instruction, gymnastics – it was all focused on one purpose: the production of citizens who were possessed of 'courage, complete obedience and physical perfection.' No mention of SEAL whatsoever, *or* thinking skills, inexplicably. To be fair, it was the physical and mental indoctrination of one of history's finest examples of Fascism, and I'm not sure that many parents these days would go for it. Although that said, we can see parallels with the perceived benefits of sending a child to military academy, presumably to have the virtues of readiness for armed conflict and enduring cold showers and cruelty.

Gods and monsters

Over in the comparatively effeminate Athens[23], the children of citizens (a relatively small, privileged class) received a school education from about seven to sixteen, in music (which included reading, writing and literature, poetry, drama), dance, gymnastics, science[24] and so on. Some then went on to a higher education to learn to be active citizens, under the direct instruction of the state. No mealy-mouthed citizenship GCSEs for them. Perhaps the past wasn't so bad after all.

This, like Spartan education, was done under the assumption that the individual was subordinate to the state: that in fact the individual

---

[20] I'd love to see a Spartan careers advisor. 'Have you thought about becoming a warrior?'

[21] At least, I hope they would.

[22] And *smoke* it.

[23] Compared to the Spartans, we're ALL effeminate.

[24] Science was *easy* then, as it had only just been invented. Sample lesson- Teacher: 'Xerxes! What causes rain?' Xerxes: 'Is it the Gods?' Teacher: 'By Zeus, you're right! Class dismissed.'

could *only* be understood in terms of their relationship to the state, and that the way we make meaning of the individual identity is by reflecting on our role and the relationships that this demands in a community. You were a father, a citizen, a soldier, a wife, a warrior before you could say what it was that you were.[25] Those roles defined you, and you derived your identity from them. As Aristotle put it, any man who could live outside society is either a god or a monster.[26]

This changed in the later Greek period, when the education of the citizen slackened off slightly to allow for greater self-identification beyond the role assigned to you in society. This was partially ushered in by a group of famous teachers known as the Sophists, who were a disorganized movement of 'professors at large' who had no common pedagogy, but who shared a common emphasis on rhetoric and the power of discussion. They believed that education should be purely useful, and were renowned (or infamous) for their tendency to teach people how to argue for any point of view, whether right or wrong. For the Sophists, utility was the aim of education. Plato teaches that one of the Sophists, Protagoras, claimed that, 'If a youth comes to me, he will learn that which he comes to learn.' Which seems innocent, until a moment's reflection shows how devilish that manifesto is for a teacher, disabling as it does the ability of the teacher to draw the student beyond what he wants to know; as if the teacher were no more than an enormous Google Search engine devoted to Satanism.

They were, of course, reviled by the traditionalists (which is a term that has a flavour of its own when we consider that were discussing matters in the millennia before the birth of Christ), like Plato and Aristotle, who thought that truth was something more than what we said it was, and education more than just the delivery of something purchased. The debate about whether education should be immediately useful and relevant, or whether it should be the process of generational inheritance, rages on still, in debates about whether schools should teach Shakespeare through the medium of rap, the medium of Twitter, or no Shakespeare at all, because what does the Bard of Stratford have to do with kids from the urban ghetto?[27]

---

[25] Which must have been tough on bums and drop-outs
[26] Or works in IT support
[27] Proponents of the 'relevance' argument seem to think inexplicably that all children live in the inner city, listen to rap music and carry guns. I believe this is untrue.

Rome, by Toutatis

Over in Italy, the Romans were busy. Not at first: the early Roman educational method was largely home-based – the mother and father raised the child, and any rudimentary schooling was undertaken at the *ludi* (from *ludus*, meaning game, which gives you some idea about how important it was seen to be). Then, having absorbed the Greek empire by 139 BC, they started to adopt its practices; elementary schools became more prevalent, and literature (all that fabulous, new, translated Greek) became intrinsic to teaching. Later on young children would be taught simple maths and writing; when they had completed this study (note: not when they simply outgrew it) they progressed to the school of the *Grammaticus*, where they were taught Greek, and especially Latin; this school was a recurrent cultural motif of the entire empire. In the fabulous and alien way of the ancient world, the study of grammar was intended to include the study of history, science, literature, music and mathematics.

These are useful and interesting sources to discuss; as we have seen, the UK educational system is, contrary to some feather-brained contemporary opinion, a relatively recent invention: free secondary education didn't get going until the 1944 act. Some claim that our educational system is Greek or Roman in origin or, more plausibly, a Victorian confection. This is then used as a criticism, implying that the way things stand in schools is dislocated from the way things are in the world. Nothing could be further from the truth, at least by the argument that our school system has geriatric, foreign chronological and cultural DNA.

Mass education is as modern as the transistor; an infant delivered in the opening years of the twentieth-century, and wiped, smacked and shown to the mother in the forties and fifties. The curriculum as we know it was designed subsequent to the 1988 Education Act, and built upon in the decade or so that followed. It can hardly be more frighteningly modern, unless we were somehow able to invent a new education system every time we opened our eyes. But I don't want to give anyone any ideas.*Et nunc reges intelligite erudimini qui judicatis terram*[28].

We see this broad pattern replicated throughout the world in many ways: Europe experienced the same broad brushstrokes in the eighteenth and nineteenth centuries as the UK did. Industrialization, urbanization, specialization, population explosions, the growth of the

---

[28] Be wise now therefore, O ye Kings: Be instructed, ye judge of the earth.

specialist, the Enlightenment focus on the individual, secularization – all affected European civilizations in similar ways with different accents.

American learning

In America, education followed similar patterns; the first waves of pilgrim immigrants formed schools that were essentially religious in character, and reflected their Lutheran, Anglican, Methodist, Baptist and Catholic origins. Education past the elementary stages was provided, as in many other countries, through private schooling and home-tutoring, and was therefore beyond the means of the majority. Education beyond the early years was also the exclusive province of the fortunate male heirs of the landed; female education at a secondary level, even for the daughters of the wealthy, was restricted, until the Woman's Republican movement started to describe the need for women also to be torch-bearers for inventing the new republic. Slight as this concession to suffragism was, it still propelled many women into the arts and humanities, even if it was for the stated purpose of breeding ladies of gentility, manners and engaging conversation, aping the English model.

The twentieth-century saw poverty and war define an era; Roosevelt, Kennedy and Eisenhower were midwives to explosive policies designed to combat the worst excesses of free-market deprivation, by enabling and mobilizing education and free schooling as a key tool of social reform, human rights and entitlement. As in other countries, utility cannot be ignored as the key factor in this movement: the need to engage and occupy an enormous segment of the population; the need to prepare a workforce; and the need to sustain and integrate an enormous community characterized by its vastness and diversity. State schooling, from its religious roots, developed a secular aim, and proselytizing became, at least nominally, prohibited.

It was Thomas Jefferson who first suggested that children should be taught in state schools, but it didn't catch on, and like their European cousins, children in America were still taught by their families, or else they had the freedom to attend any one of a number of fee-paying private schools. Annoyingly enough for exponents of the division between religion and education, it was, as usual, religious bodies such as the Puritans who instituted free education for the common child, on local scales. Secularists later adopted a 'we'll take it from here' attitude, but in a pre-welfare society, it was often only the church that offered a few crumbs to the poor and the peripheral.

It wasn't until 1852 in Massachusetts that the first compulsory schools were instituted, and it took until 1918 for all states to provide this (the last being New York, incidentally), and in some cases at an elementary level only. But schools were still segregated, and black Americans had to wait until 1954 and Brown vs the Board of Education to sit in partnership with their white peers. Most schools in America now operate with little federal intervention, so the majority of administration and direction operates at a county level, controlling the 15,000 school districts. Fifty million children now enjoy state education in this context, and because of various guarantees of independence there is wide variation between curricula and content. Surprisingly, there is an enormous shortage of teaching staff (2.2 million vacancies in 2010), particularly in inner-city schools in poorer areas.

In 2002, George Bush signed the famous No Child Left Behind Act[29] in response to the 1983 report 'A nation at risk'[30] which predicted that America would fall behind other nations in crucial literacy and numeracy skills.[31] As a result, all state schools were required to publish standardized examination results in those areas, calling some to claim that schools were being forced to teach to the test too much, at the expense of the broader aims of education. Proponents of the Act claimed that it was an invaluable diagnostic tool for identifying failing schools, and a powerful method for 'encouraging' those schools to improve.[32] American schooling, with its enormous scope and scale, offers a fascinating mirror to other countries through its sheer diversity of populations, management structures and variability of curricular approaches. As one of the largest providers of state education in the world, it provides the rest of the liberal democratic nations an interesting reflection of the challenges faced by countries intent on social reform and the delivery of perceived human rights in the context of a state balanced between the free market and interventionist authority.

---

[29] Where do they GET these names?
[30] Not in any hurry, clearly
[31] This is a meme that you'll hear a lot in education – 'they're catching up!' etc.
[32] 'Encourage' is a broad term, of course. As Gore Vidal nearly said, sometimes it is useful for words to reverse their meaning from time to time.

Germany

After the Weimar republic (1919–1934), Germany saw a compulsory programme of elementary education, *Grundschule*, which provided a four-year grounding in the foundational skills, which was followed by a six-year secondary provision, the *Aufbauschule*, which was broadly liberal in concept. With the rise of Nazism came the belief in the *Volksstaat*, the idea that the individual must be subordinated to the state in a way that Plato might have approved of, had he been a total bastard. The state became the only authorized body for the provision of education; city children spent an extra year (the *Landjahr*) being indoctrinated and working in rural environments; Adolf Hitler Schools were instigated (I'm not making this up, unfortunately); school curricula were modelled on Nazi ideology, including an emphasis on eugenics, phrenology and other pseudosciences, which shows that science has a history of being used to promote shameless, baseless ideological causes.

After the post-war reorganization, German schools now broadly follow the same model: a *Grundschule*, a *Mittelschule* and a variety of secondaries that are answerable to the local state, leading to University for some. Provision is a mixture of state, free (in the majority) and private provision, as in other European models.

France

Interestingly enough, Napoleon was very interested in state schooling, especially secondary; like many emperors, he saw the opportunity for indoctrination. And in a frightening nod to modernity, he instituted school inspectors to monitor the orthodoxy of such schools; he also instituted the training of teachers in the so-called 'normal' schools, a project that continued in many other countries … eventually. After Napoleon got the chop in 1815, the state returned its attention to elementary education, where students were taught in upper and lower primaries; the curriculum included maths, French,[33] religion and in the upper years, such treats as geography and science.

Fees were payable by families who could afford to pay: universal entitlement was some way off yet, and attendance was not compulsory. In 1881, education was made compulsory and free to all children between the ages of six and thirteen, and religion was dislocated

---

[33] Fancy that.

from state education. Private education was finally allowed after 1886, mostly for Catholic schools. It wasn't until 1930 that secondary education became free from fees. The great curriculum discussion of the twentieth-century was the eternal debate between the classics (Greek, Latin, Classical History) and the Modern subjects (such as science, geography); it always seems odd to see such subjects classified as modern, but in the great scheme of civilization, they can be seen as relative upstarts in the field. See: sociology, psychology, citizenship, which amusingly enough have Greek names. Ironically.

Now we have seen how education evolved from the ancient to the modern worlds, we can see that centrally controlled schools, specially trained teachers, criteria, targets and even universal entitlement are very modern beasts. Now that such things are landmarks in the landscape of education, and now that we exist in a world of regulation, prescription and accountability, it would be prudent to turn to another question: how is educational policy made? Who makes the decisions about education that affect teachers and presumably you? And how do they make these decisions? The answers might surprise you.

3 How Policy is Made

‘ THE SACRED DATA IS PURE !
THIS IS CLEAR EVIDENCE ! ’

EDUCATIONAL RESEARCH .

You might think that, by now, all decisions about teaching had been made after pooling the collective wisdom of the teaching centuries. You would be wrong. Distressingly, a huge number of decisions about how we teach, what we teach and why we teach are reached through means that I can only describe as arbitrary (at best) and careless (if I'm being more honest). In 2010, the CfBT Education Trust wrote a paper on the ways in which ministers make decisions in education: *Instinct or Reason: How education policy is made and how we might make it better* by Adrian Perry, Christian Amadeo, Mick Fletcher and Elizabeth Walker.

It conducted a substantial literature review of memoirs and auto-biographies, and interviewed many major figures from the policy establishment (education ministers and relevant junior ministers). It identified several key factors as significant in the process of policy formation in education, and makes for sobering reading for anyone who hoped that the people who make the big decisions know more about education than anyone else. As you're reading this, remember that these are the people who run education.

1. Urgency

Many ministers and decision-makers often act because 'something must be done', perhaps in response to new information, or the presentation of old material as new. An example would be following the release of annual Ofsted data which revealed that schools in a particular area were underperforming; or that the number of young adults Not In Education or Employment (NEETs) had soared in a given context. These types of scenarios, ministers admitted, seemed to present an urgent need to take action.

2. The ideology of policy makers

Naturally one might intuitively think that the personal political beliefs of the policy makers would play an important part in the production of policy. One of the biggest ideological shifts that has taken place in the last thirty years in the UK has been the marketi-zation of political discourse across a wide spectrum of areas. Bringing the values of the business sector – 'New Public Management' – has resulted in a broad difference in the ways that policy problems and their solutions have been phrased, and therefore interpreted. Choice has become paramount, and schools have been seen as delivery mechanisms for a product (education) to consumers. Transparency has been key to this process of choice, and school inspection reports, league tables and other articles of quantitative data analysis have become key for parents and government in forming opinions and decisions about the utility of schools, teachers and teaching methods.

3. International comparisons

Ministers find it useful to rely on models of education exemplified by other countries and states. On the one hand, this can be a useful comparative analysis, and saves policy-makers from investing in large-scale projects, which are costly and time-consuming, and research, which can share these problems. The data are already there; the projects are already running, and ministers can simply judge if those models are desirable. On the other hand, comparative analysis is fraught with methodological problems: is like being compared with like? Cultural and economic context is often vital in order to understand the success of any initiative and, to speak plainly, what works in one country may not do so in another.

The example quoted is that of Free Schools in Finland, which may (or may not) result in higher grade averages. This comparison has been used as an argument in favour of Free Schools in the UK. But commentators have noted that one significant difference between Finland and the UK is the relatively high status enjoyed by teachers in Finland, with concomitant dividends in pupil behaviour and quality levels of teacher training/ candidates.

4. Cost

No minister or decision-maker can ignore this factor, and they face a perpetual battle to justify projects, often on a principle of utility, the hidden costs of *not* undertaking the project, the larger economic climate or the utility of competing projects.Of course, decisions based on economic reasons are prey to the vice of measurement – anything that cannot produce a clear, quantitative result suffers in this process. The result is a focus on objectives that can, like GCSE averages, be mathematically described. I probably don't need to tell you how much in our lives we consider to be valuable, but cannot be directly measured.

5. Electoral popularity

Ministers and decision-makers do not enjoy tenure, and they are painfully aware of the potential impact each decision will have on the opinion of the electorate. A clear example of this is the *Every Child Matters* initiative which was a (some would say rushed)[1] raft of legislation in response to the public outcry over the death of Victoria Climbie, who died despite the efforts of several public sector agencies. In this context, the media plays a huge part. The 1988 Education Reform Act was eased into the realm of public opinion by sympathetic newspapers who highlighted the (imaginary) excesses of 'loony left' Local Authorities who were portrayed as excessively ideologically left-wing, and out of touch with public consensus. The Tomlinson Report, which recommended significant changes to the award system at Key Stages four and five, was ignored by the incumbent government, because of fears that the public would react strongly to an 'attack' on A-levels, the perceived[2] Gold Standard of education.

6. Pressure from influential groups

It is clear that some influences and stakeholders in education are more equal than others. Business leaders and University Vice-Chancellors have much more impact on the development of policy than to local authorities or Trade Unions. Religious groups still retain a strong influence, as evidenced by the privileged position they enjoy concerning selectivity.

7. Personal experience

Many ministers indicated that they were guided in their policy decisions by factors such as their own experiences in education (everyone has, after all, been to school) and the experiences of close friends, family and neighbours. Tony Blair, for example, was allegedly hostile to local government involvement based on the experiences of his children. David Cameron has been vocal about his concerns over Special Needs education subsequent to his own

---

[1] For instance, by me.
[2] I use the word carefully.

experiences with his son. David Blunkett allegedly supported the policy of inclusion because of his experiences in a Special School as a blind child.The glaring problem with this factor is that very few ministers or Prime Ministers have ever experienced the inside of a state school unless they were cutting the ribbon to open it. And as Anthony Flew famously pointed out with his Black Swan problem, it is always dangerous to universalize, to generalize from a particular or a specific. I was once bitten by a dog. Do all dogs bite?

8. Research evidence

Decision-makers have access to huge amounts of data and research.[3] But it is clear from interview and literature review that this plays a less significant role in the decision process than the other factors listed, and when it does pay a role, it is mediated by a variety of factors. Many ministers stated that they held a belief about a given policy, and then sought evidence to back it up. Quite apart from the misapprehension this shows about what constitutes responsible evidence-based policy, it also reveals the difficulty of knowing which evidence to use when different studies often apparently conflict, or point to seemingly opposite conclusions. Another factor is that research, even carefully conducted, does not always provide a clear recipe to resolve the imagined problems it claims to uncover. There may be an irresolvable fact/value gap between statements of fact and statements of value, or the problem of the naturalistic fallacy, as G. E. Moore might put it. Simply knowing the way things are does not immediately present a solution to the problem 'how should things be'.

This shows us how spontaneous, how personal the decision-making process is. They are all – I repeat ALL – contestable. They are all passed on to the profession as dogma and fact. Did I mention that the world of education has become a racket?

So is the problem that the people in charge of what teachers actually have to do don't use enough research? Unfortunately it's not that simple either. Research is often the weapon used *against* teachers.

---

[3] Every page of it a hoot, I assure you.

Educational research: can science save education?

Surely we can turn to the laboratory to solve the great questions of education? This was the great nineteenth-century project, after science had made such startling inroads into understanding and solving the problems of the natural world – chemistry, biology and physics had all produced miracles. It seemed that the empirical method of study – observe, hypothesize, test – held the answers to all our ills. Imagine what could be done if we were to turn this mighty organ on to the problems of the social sphere. One of those spheres was, inevitably, education. And believe me, there is a lot of science available on it – whole faculties are now devoted to the study of every aspect of the workings of education. One might hope that this project had borne fruit, but the results have been far from conclusive.

So let's take as an example one simple question: does giving schools more money improve education, or does it not? The answer seems obvious, but is it?

A BBC report from the 14th of January 2011 looked at the evidence: 'A recent Pisa study from the OECD compared academic performance across a wide range of countries and offered some support for the government's view that money is not a key factor. Another study, by Francois Leclerque for UNESCO in 2005, surveyed a wide range of other economists' attempts to find a correlation between resources and results. Some found a positive correlation. Others found the opposite. Leclerque concluded that, whichever view you took, it was as much a matter of one's previous belief and opinion as it was of scientific knowledge. One major study (by Hanushek and Kimko, 2000) looked at pupils' international maths scores and compared them to several different measures of school spending. It is not clear whether spending more on schools leads to better results. Their conclusion was: "The overall story is that variations in school resources do not have strong effects on test performance."'[4]

So that's all perfectly clear then. At least we have all the data we need to make a decision. Not.

Think about what's happening here: tens of millions of pounds spent, an equivalent proportion of academic labour, the finest minds in education, all focused on one point, one question, like shining a million light bulbs on to a spot and turning it into a laser. Only to find that all you have is a very bright room, and an army of moths dive-bombing the window.

---

[4] www.bbc.c.uk/news/education-12175480

The desire to apply the methods of the natural sciences to the social sphere is entirely understandable; after all, the benefits that have been obtained from the laboratories and notebooks of the men in white coats have given long life, comfort, leisure time and, most importantly, television and *Mad Men*. Imagine the benefits we could glean if we turned our microscopes and astrolabes away from covalent bonds and meteorological taxonomy and towards the thing we love and value most: ourselves. Cue: psychology, anthropology, history, politics, educational theory, etc. Now all we have to do is send out the scientists, and sit back and wait for all those lovely data to be turned into the cure for sadness, the end to war, the answer to life's meaning and while you're at it, how best to teach children.

And yet, here we are, still waiting. The example I gave at the start of this section serves as just one illustration. For every study you produce that demonstrates red ink lowers pupil motivation, or brings them out in hives or something, I can show you a study that says, no, it's *green* ink that does the trick. For any survey that shows the benefits of group work, there are equivalent surveys that say the same about project work, or individual work, or the Montessori method, or learning in zero gravity or whatever. It is, to be frank, maddening, especially if you're a teacher and on the receiving end of every new initiative and research-inspired gamble that comes along. The effect is not dissimilar to being at the foot of an enormous well and wondering not if, but *how many* buckets of dog turds will rain on you that day, and how many soufflés you'll be expected to make out of it. To quote Manzi:[5]

'Unlike physics or biology, *the social sciences have not demonstrated the capacity to produce a substantial body of useful, nonobvious, and reliable predictive rules about what they study* – that is, human social behaviour, including the impact of proposed government programs. *The missing ingredient is controlled experimentation,* which is what allows science positively to settle certain kinds of debates.'[6]

And that, I think, summarizes the problems teaching has with the terrifying deluge of educational research that has emerged in the twentieth-century and beyond, and the apparently awful advice that has drenched the education sector for decades with its well-intentioned but essentially childish misunderstandings.

A priori, the social scientific method is best used as a commentary on human beings and their behaviour, not as a predictive or reductive mechanism. So the next time you read another piece of educational

---

[5] http://www.city-journal.org/2010/20_3_social-science.html
[6] Emphases my own.

research hitting *Breakfast TV*, feel free to say, 'Oh really? That's interesting.' But make sure you hold your breath. And get your umbrella and saucepan out.

Aristotle's view of *nous* is relevant here. This is a cognitive ability, a kind of 'practical wisdom' that a teacher needs to practise in the professional classroom. It struggles to flourish if the practitioner is constrained by a variety of rather rubbish external recommendations and 'best practices'. For example, broad guidelines can never replace sensitivity to context as the best guide to handle behaviour management. Of course, there is clearly a place for rules, particularly in large-scale institutions that need to have shared values and a degree of consensus regarding behavioural norms, sanctions and rewards. But rules must be used when they are useful, and suspended when they are not. Or, more specifically, all systems of law need to have areas where personal interpretation is possible, in the same way that a judge must sentence according to guidelines, but can operate freely within them.

The absence of the teaching professional from the process of consultation, research and policy creation is one of the most glaring deficiencies in the modern educational community. Redressing this imbalance will take a great deal of will on the part of the teaching profession and its representatives, who have seemingly lost the capacity to imagine themselves as meaningful. I suggest that if the teaching community expects the educational establishment to induct it back into the political process, it may endure a long wait. Teachers should be more than delivery mechanisms.

Anything goes?

Not at all. Just because a lot of social science is abused and tormented into supporting the latest fashionable educational ideas doesn't mean that in the absence of certainty we should revert to superstition and lawlessness, any more than the lack of total certainty in the biological sciences should prevent us from relying on chemistry that seems to soothe in clinical trials rather than sting. I've indicated that a good teacher needs to be able to trust two things:

1. the experience of other experienced teachers
2. the experience of their own eyes.

Both of these can be understood using educational research; educational theory can inspire and converse with the sum total of the teacher experience, but it should never overrule it in a way that presents as counterintuitive, any more than Mao Zedong should have been allowed to get his hands on the Chinese national economy in five-year bites because 'that's what Marx thought'. Experience trumps theory in teaching. Remember that. If you find that children respond (and they do) to firm discipline seasoned with manners and concern and inspired by compassion, then don't throw your detention slips out of the window as soon as you read the latest hopelessly optimistic thesis on children's motivation that suggests they respond more warmly to promises of cream eggs and cuddles.

The intellectual vacuum in teaching is filled by opinion

Teaching has survived in the same shape for centuries; this infuriates some, who are still waiting for the revolution in the educational sphere as happened in the surgical one. This infuriates some, who demand that the paradigm be turned on its head to allow exciting new models of education to rise, ones that fit the brave new world of social networks, cyber-societies, child rights and smart drugs.

What is the point of this constant invention, reinvention and upset? To enable twenty-first-century learning, we are told. And what might that even look like? And what was so wrong with the existing model? Every professor in Cambridge and Oxford, I imagine, probably enjoyed a fairly traditional classroom environment. This insistence that the wheel must be reinvented is a chase for the Questing Beast: pointless and trivial. Humans are biologically identical to our Bronze Age ancestors; our brains work in the same way. Our societies, although apparently brand new and unique, are inventive reinterpretations of what has gone before. If someone wants to suggest a 'whole new way' of learning to me, I'll treat them with the same caution as someone telling me they've thought of a 'whole new way of eating'. Especially if their new way involves me parting with my credit card details.

The Shark and the Teacher; closer than you think

So too in education. Teaching practice has occupied a relatively stable space for centuries because there has been no immediate pressure to change for any reason. The teacher leads the lesson, possessed of good content knowledge and skill, and commands a room full of children who must be amenable to the reasonable wishes of the pedagogue. These students listen, write, repeat and reflect upon what the teacher has instructed. The teacher, as an expert, then evaluates how he or she thinks they have performed. It really is as simple as that, at least in the basics, and any attempt to monkey around with that format would be tantamount to suggesting that a shark be given an outboard motor in order to raise the bar on its fish quotient.

But if you turn around, you will see a number of desk educationalists attempting to strap just such a gadget on to you, and other more unpleasant fixtures, anywhere they can reach. The last thirty years in education have seen an enormous intervention by people who just couldn't keep their hands out of the biscuit tin. Every new government loves to play with the Big Education Ball, because it is only in the demographic of the under-eighteens that attempts to win the hearts and minds of people can be so extreme. Put simply, you can push a child a lot further than an adult, because they don't vote, and are less likely to associate their school privations with a political party.

Education has become a racket

Understanding this a little will help to understand why there has been such an obsession in education for reform, dazzling and brainless in its speed, breadth and effect. We, as teachers, need to be alive to this in every way we can; when we are trained, when we are asked to adopt yet another mission statement, and when we are being evaluated. The revolution that classrooms really need will be a long time coming. Until the day that a representative body actually represents the interests of both teachers and children, or until the day that ministers and teachers work together meaningfully, it needs to happen with teachers themselves, and we need to make it happen. It needs to happen in your classroom, starting tomorrow, and it needs to happen for the rest of our careers.

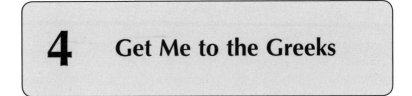

4   Get Me to the Greeks

The Philosophy of Teaching

'OFSTED VISITS ARISTOTLE'S LYCEUM.'

'UNSATISFACTORY??'

How do we teach teachers?

The TES behaviour forum taught me that everyone wanted to know what to *do*; and I can testify that, in a school environment, theory is as helpful as sandpaper on piles; action is all, and inaction results in the incineration of your ego. I was getting quite handy at telling teachers what I thought they should do in each situation. But how did *I* know? The clue lay in something that should have noticed earlier. Questions often went like this:

> Dear Tom
>
> One boy in my Year 6 class is refusing to do anything I say, even though he knows that if I report him he'll lose half a second of Golden Time and be looked at sternly for a heartbeat by someone he doesn't know.
>   Now I'm worried that I'll never be a good teacher and that I'm completely rubbish. Help!
>
> Worried

They don't know what to do; so they think that they themselves are bad, inefficient, corrupt. They internalize their lack of skill as a personal flaw. But you don't know what you don't know. It's the lesson we learn from Bilbo Baggins' killer question to Gollum that wins him the One Ring, in what might be the least fair test of wits in literary history: What's in my pocket?[1] If you don't know, you don't know. Who can blame you for that?

Virtue Ethics and teaching

You can't have rules that prescribe every situation in the classroom; but nor can you make it up as you go along. But there is a third possibility for those wishing to become good or better teachers; the Virtue Ethics approach. It focuses on developing a good character *character*. This sounds strange to our modern ears, because we are so used to following rules, or working out the best outcomes for us whenever we consider a choice of actions. Virtue Ethics has an ancient heritage,

---

[1] If I was Gollum, I'd have spannered the pedantic little hairdresser. Call that a question?

but has enjoyed a late twentieth-century revival. It states that more important than rules and outcomes: is your character what sort of person are you?

Example: imagine a brutal murderer/ thief, banged up in the maximum security wing of some remote prison. The prison is state of the art, CCTV every five yards, and the whole wing is surrounded by armed sentries high above them, with orders to shoot if any trouble breaks out; this is the constant environment that the prisoners live in. You can imagine that our protagonist toes the line pretty much all the time; he knows that if he does, he gets yard privileges and work in the library; and if he doesn't, his brains get to rag roll the walls. He may, therefore, be perfectly well behaved, every minute of the day. But would you say you trusted him? Would you turn your back on him if he was let out for a day? Of course not. Why? Because you ascribe more vicious tendencies to his character; you would say he is cruel; brutal; selfish. His character was rotten.

And that's how we can make a link between character and behaviour. We say that a man with character x has the disposition to behave in a certain way x given the opportunity to do so. I can summarize this in one sentence:

Behaviour flows from character

This little line summarizes everything I need to say about Virtue Ethics, the third approach. In essence, teachers need to focus on developing a good teacher character. It's a theory that relies on experience, that relies on good teacher trainers, but also relies on teachers wanting to be good teachers, rather than just doing what they think the rule book tells them.

This method isn't easy; it takes time and thought and reflection. Neither is it supposed to be used instead of following the rules – the rules must be learned and, in most cases, adhered to. But what it is is a method for teachers to focus on themselves as people, and as professionals – a word that is rapidly losing its meaning in an increasingly didactic and prescribed career. It demands that we work on ourselves, in a workout no less important or intensive than any costly monthly programme with a personal trainer down at the gym. The difference is that this approach won't cost you anything, and you can practise the exercises all the time. The goal is to make you a better teacher, and that's going to take a lot of work because it's not an easy task.

Just to make it seem even easier, there will never come a point when you relax and think, 'I've made it as a teacher – now I can take it easy.' Teaching is an experience of lifelong learning, and so it should be, because learning is a dynamic experience that involves change and movement. As soon as you stop learning as a teacher, you start to slide backwards. There is no treading water, except at the most rudimentary level. I've seen teachers who have been in the profession for twenty-five years who still couldn't manage a class or teach an interesting lesson. Think about that – twenty-five years. I remember one such stalwart said to me, 'I've got over twenty years experience – you'd think they'd listen to me.' I thought to myself, 'No you don't mate; you've got one year's experience twenty times.'

The Teacher Workout

Working on your teaching character involves four steps:

1. identifying the virtues you need to improve
2. choosing situations where you can practise those virtues
3. reflecting on your experience, preferably with a mentor
4. trying again.

It's not nuclear physics, and in many ways it reflects what you might do already in a piecemeal way; but this approach makes it much more focused on developing characteristics that stay with you, so that whenever you encounter a new situation, or a variation of an old one, your character kicks in and guides you to the right solution. Remember: behaviour flows from character.

The next section is devoted to understanding what kind of characteristics and virtues you need to have in order to be a successful teacher. For some of you, these virtues will already be innate, and simply need to be reinforced in an educational setting. Even then, there will be a readjustment period, while you learn to tailor your responses to the specific needs of the environment. When I entered teaching, I had pretty solid confidence in speaking to large crowds of drunk strangers; trying to talk to a large class of children was slightly easier because of this experience, but it still wasn't a proper safety net for the vertiginous spotlight that only teaching can involve. It takes time to build up the particular muscles relevant to the exercise.

The Doctrine of the Mean

These are the virtues that teachers need to have; with these virtues we can do the job that we need to do. Aristotle described how merely possessing virtues wasn't enough – it was necessary to display the correct amount of the virtue, for the right duration, at the right time. To illustrate: a popular virtue that people tend to need throughout life would be bravery. But bravery, by itself, cannot be intrinsically good; for example, we can imagine situations where one could be too brave.

Example:

You're in a bar. Beside you are a dozen Hells Angels; evidently their favourite team has just lost a game, and they aren't happy. One of them spills your pint. Do you:

a) apologize for your clumsiness and offer to buy him another one?
b) say nothing?
c) announce in a loud voice, 'Which one of you Tricycle-driving fairies wants to dance first?'

If you said (c) then I applaud your insane levels of confidence. You won't hear my applause because you'll be a thin layer of jam on the bar floor,[2] but there we go. You can obviously be *too* brave. Aristotle spotted this problem; he instructed us to obey the Doctrine of the Mean: display the appropriate level of virtue at the right time. Sometimes high levels of bravery are required – high-wire walking from the top of a burning skyscraper is the obvious, everyday example that springs to mind. But in the example above, you may actually consider it wise to keep a lid on all that confidence, and acknowledge the battles that can't be won.

How do we understand the Doctrine of the Mean? How do we understand what the right level of bravery would be, and for what length of time? The simple answer is that there is no simple answer, nor should we expect there to be. Virtue Ethics is a curious moral system: it demands that we consider every situation as a new opportunity to understand what doing the right thing in every circumstance would be. It demands, in short, that we be adults, and the best way to understand it is by asking yourself these questions:

---

[2] And I'll be in a taxi by the time you speak the last syllable.

1. who am I?
2. what is my role in the community?
3. what virtue (and how much) would aid my success in this situation?

Put this way, it becomes a little simpler. If I see a fire, my choice of action is clear if I'm a fireman; so too are the virtues I need to possess in order to execute my duties.

The point is that there is no definitive answer to 'what should I do?' in any moral situation – and I should point out that Virtue Ethics perceives every action as a moral one, including ones we might think trivial. Everything we choose to do or not to do is an example of character in motion, and as such has a moral content. Deciding to have Weetabix over Cheerios is a moral act, simply because it has consequences for others, and shows an internal preference that however infinitesimally displays my character.

So how do we apply this to teaching? Let's return to the questions: 1. Who am I? That's the easy one – you're the educator; you're the teacher. You flourish when they flourish; they flourish when you flourish. Isn't that beautiful? If you're a good teacher, they become better students; if they are good students, they help you to be a better teacher. I could weep at the thought. Of course it doesn't often go that smoothly, but you get the idea. This is why it's so important to settle the question of what the aim of the teacher is; because if you think that your aim is to make them happy, then you'll need one set of virtues and characteristics – a warm heart, a red nose, and a quilted jacket with large pockets full of confetti, I should think. But if your aim is to teach them, then you'll need another set, which I'll expand on in the next section.

It's important to have a clear, rather muscular idea of what your role is. I have wailed and gnashed my teeth like Pharaoh's slaves at the sight, time after time, of new teachers entering a classroom, tiptoeing around the children and being driven from the room by a class of baying, uncontrolled teenagers, simply because the teacher wasn't clear what they were supposed to be doing. It's the same cry I hear on the Behaviour forums of the TES, day in and day out. What should I do? A kid told me to fuck off. What should I do?

And it brings me back to the day, years ago, when I took a young madam from the room because she was essentially a screechy, unpleasant carbuncle on the face of creation. 'Who the FUCK do you think you are?' she asked, sweetly. 'Telling me to leave the room. Who the FUCK!'

Well now, I know exactly who I am; I'm the teacher. And so, I think, are you.

It's an awesome responsibility; I don't make a claim to it being a profession lightly. A lot of gas is passed about this; we're a profession all right, but there are often times when I fail to see much professionalism, and it only makes the case for our status a lot harder. If we expect professional status, then we need to raise our game. Marx would undoubtedly recognize this as what he would call 'raising consciousness'. We need, en masse, to start to perceive ourselves as teachers, and consider what that means. I've had it up to my gills with helpless, lazy staff bemoaning the fact that the kids were rude and surly to them. Do something about it! If they have, then their downfall at least comes from other sources. But until every teacher has exhausted every opportunity open to them in the classroom, it's not yet time to shrug the shoulders and say, 'Kids are horrible, aren't they?' No they aren't. They're just kids, just like we were. The difference is that we have lost sight of who we are, and the kids, sensing this, have perhaps naturally risen to fill the void of authority that we unwittingly vacated. There's another phrase for this: man up.

The virtues I'll discuss are, in no particular order:

◆ **Courage**
◆ **Wisdom**
◆ **Patience**
◆ **Compassion**
◆ **Justice**

Notice that I don't claim that you have to have these characteristics in abundance. What I'll seek to show is that these virtues will all be required in differing quantities, at different times. Remember when I suggested that you could be too brave? The same goes for all the others. At times you will have to restrain your tendency to display compassion or kindness, a fact I learned the first time I had to deworm a cat.

You, as a professional, need to be responsible for your own education in a way that is tragic, given the enormous importance of your role. I task you to educate yourself; to enter classrooms and think about what worked, and what didn't; to provide yourself with the data you need to construct your own experiments; to develop your own style; your own personality, and not the serving suggestion of the men from the ministry.

A teacher is an academic, a professional and a craftsman. An academic, because he is the harbinger of the past, and the conduit to the future of the intellectual inheritance of history; a professional because there are standards and duties inherent in the role that deserve a nearly sacred execution; and a craftsman because so much of the role is a craft, learned on the job, absorbed osmotically through movement and repetition, by encounter, by conversation, by the smooth repetition of arms, legs and mouth until the innumerable sequences and combinations of reactions and actions are apprehended intuitively.

A carpenter considers, on a conscious level, how he will approach a task; but there is a deeper, non-conscious level of understanding about how to hold the chisel, the hammer, that is more akin to knowing how to balance. It isn't a collection of facts or data. It's *understanding*. Some of it is knowledge. That's why there is only so much a book like this (or any book – don't send this one back, please) can tell you. But what I can do is to try to present the experience of teaching in a novel way; to help you to reflect; at least to understand that you are in charge of your teaching, and that you aren't bound by the rulebooks of the iniquitous and orthodox. You can be the unconventional teacher who has his class rapt with awe; or you can be the silent disciplinarian; or the generous mentor; or a million other paradigms.

There as many different teachers you can be as there are people on the planet. Your interpretation of these virtues is more like jazz than Gregorian Chant.

Good luck.

Section Two: The Qualities of a Great Teacher – Developing Your Teaching Character

Ofsted is at your school
1 min ago. Comment. Like.

👍 Everyone else likes this

School man that sucks
1 min ago

Other school Not ready?
1 min ago

School No lesson plans, no
schemes of work...FML.

Other school Sucks to be
you.

Ofsted Cheers for
that! Outside your room.

School. What? Sonova..
Just now.

To Aristotle, there were many virtues; virtues of the mind (like
intelligence, knowledge and memory), virtues of the body (such as
dexterity, strength and my favourite one of all, a deep voice), and
virtues of character, such as courage, forbearance and temperance.

It's the last of these three types that concerns us here. Physically you should be as fit as you can be, so as not to impede the execution of your role; a state of good health also helps to keep the mind clear and the emotions under check. But I'll leave that to you, as this isn't a book about low-fat diets, crunch curls and giving up the gaspers. I know that, as a teacher, you will already be possessed of a physique that would make men and women alike swoon. I'll take that as a given.

I'll come back to memory, knowledge and craft later on. For now I want to focus on the virtues of character. Your character I can describe simply as the sort of person you are, and how others might describe you. Are you kind, mean, tardy, reliable, randy or gregarious? Perhaps you are all of these things at once, like Bill Clinton. For Aristotle, a virtue was defined as the correct amount of one of these characteristics at the appropriate time. Too much of any characteristic was an excess. Too little was a deficiency. Having a virtue was a sign that a man was flourishing, experiencing what the Greeks called *eudemonia* – a happiness of soul, body and mind. Not happiness-as-pleasure, but happiness as fulfilment; being the best a person can be. You can see some of these qualities, and their unscrupulous outlying descriptors, below:

Justice

Aquinas once said that he knew exactly what time was – until you asked him to give a definition of it. This is exactly how we approach the idea of justice. At first sight, everyone know what it is. Even a small child knows to howl when some accrued benefit is denied; even the meanest of children (or perhaps because they are mean) have hypersensitive radar for justice, or more particularly its absence. 'That's not fair!' is a cry that any parent recognizes as immediately as a pimple on the inside of one's eyelid. OK, so what is justice?

And the problems begin.

Justice is fairness, or in other words when we receive what we deserve. Life, it has often been pointed out, isn't terribly fair, in that there appears to be no self-correcting function of the universe to regulate the correct allocation of desert (or even desserts, which are frequently unfairly allocated in my experience). But to many that's OK, because their religion guarantees them a reckoning in the hereafter, which I suppose must be one of the main perks of membership (or not, if you follow the faith; God will cut you down whether you believe in him or not. I'm not qualified to say, and it exceeds my brief anyway: see my follow up book: 'Ultimate Questions for Dummies'). That's the Abrahamic faiths anyway; creeds more Oriental hold a cyclical view of life, encapsulated for some in the famously misunderstood idea of karma, which can briefly be described as the law that governs the journey from one life to the next. If you act well and correctly, you enjoy an improvement in the *next* life, not in this one. Whenever I see an old hippie watch the downfall of an unpleasant man and say, 'That's karma, man,' I feel like spannering them.[1] Karma doesn't apply intra-life; it's strictly a border toll. You can be a complete shit throughout your life and still prosper like a family of fruit flies in a room full of ripe bananas.

Justice sometimes seems in short supply in our lives. In other words, it raineth on the just and the unjust alike, and sometimes it's the bad guys who have all the brollies. I know. I have one.

The source of this idea we have of justice is a fascinating question, as is seeking the source of any of the rivers of ethics by which we live. But for our purposes it is enough to say that a thirst for justice exists, perhaps within us all. So what do we mean when we say justice?

Imagine a cake. Imagine me and you[2] and eight other beautiful strangers in the room where a cake has been delivered. Next to the cake there is a knife (this is beginning to sound like one of those old pre-Xbox text adventures for the BBC Micro),[3] and you want to cut the cake up. What would be a fair way to divide it?

If you said 'into ten pieces,' you would have provided a perfectly reasonable answer.[4] But why is that fair? Because it's equal, you might say. And I could as easily reply by saying, why is equality fair? Because no one receives more than any other? That's merely a redefinition of equality. So I'll say it again: why is equality fair?

Let me complicate our cosy cake/justice party. What if someone there is starving to death? Would it be fair if we all got equal shares? What if one of us were diabetic? What if I had made the cake; wouldn't I deserve more to recognise my contribution? What if – whisper it – it was someone's birthday?

---

[1] Which would probably screw up my Karma something terrible.
[2] I do.
[3] Go north: you can't do that. Bite lip, etc...
[4] Apart from the fact that nobody- and I mean nobody- knows how to cut a cake into ten equal pieces. I know; I used to be a waiter in a theme restaurant – or *dinertainment* – where such cakes were regularly butchered into a powdery crumb-bath. Oh the humanity. The *marzipan*.

I was once – in a previous life, where my karma was pretty much screwed – a waiter. I had the hellish displeasure to be serving a party of twelve churlish ten-year-old girls, at a birthday party. The birthday girl was vile, truly loathsome and repellent. And there was a little girl at the far end to whom everyone was alternately ignoring or being spiteful; she was plump and gauche, and if ever a girl had been invited to a party solely to please someone's mother, she it was. Her presence was only tolerated by virtue of her doubling as a human piñata. After half an hour of watching her get socially crucified, I decided I'd had enough, and decided the scales of the Universe needed a little redressing, so I gave her a balloon and chatted to her. The birthday girl immediately got cross, and said to me, 'Don't speak to her, she smells. Why does she get a balloon?' To which I replied, 'Because life isn't fair.'[5]

Fair doesn't mean everyone being treated equally, although we may value equality – they aren't the same thing. Aristotle said that to treat people equally who were not equal was itself unjust. For instance, the little girl I tried to cheer up wasn't in the same position as her vile peers – she was the victim. A man with diamond shoes doesn't need charity. A tall man doesn't need a booster seat. A childless woman doesn't need nappies. Am I going too fast? The fair allocation of justice doesn't entail that all are treated equally IF there is a reasonable cause to presume an existing inequality.

Does this mean that, in order to treat people with justice, you can treat them differently? Yes. And no.[6]

You set homework for a class of twenty-five students. One of the kids comes up to you and says, 'Can we just pretend this homework didn't happen?' You say, 'No.' Of course you do; it would be completely unfair to let the joker off homework because there isn't a discernable difference that shows that an inequality needs to be redressed. The child may be different from his peers in a million ways, of course (I'm hoping, unless you teach a laboratory of clones), but the point is that from the perspective of a teacher, he's the same as the other students.

Take the same example. This time, you know that the child has to be taken into care over the weekend; or has broken their arm; or looks after a parent; or any number of differences. Now we have a difference that shows some level of inequality that can be redressed

---

[5] These are the very least of my sins.
[6] You're welcome.

by your intervention. The difference this time is meaningful; it relates to the decision you make. And this is why justice is such a vital ingredient in the repertoire of a teacher. Children are HYPERsensitive to justice; they discern differentiation like .... rats with special radar for it. Particularly when they inhabit the lighter side of the scales. Funnily enough, kids (and adults, their taller counterparts) rarely cry foul when the wheel of fortune lands them on the jackpot. Perhaps our sense of justice is blunted in some way by prosperity. It may well be true. It is rare, in my experience, to see armies of millionaires marching down Whitehall protesting about how dreadfully unfair the world is, and what do we want? Social justice! etc. Usually it's the less fragrant members of society.

If you were trying to alienate and annoy children- if you were, for some kamikaze/lemming reason, in the mood to see exactly how quickly you could piss the kids off to the point where they refuse to even breathe if you ask them, then simply do this; be arbitrary. Be unfair. Treat some as favourites for no discernible reason, and others as enemies with equally random justification. Watch how quickly they start to hate you with a vigour that can actually be weighed by a set of kitchen scales. Not long, I promise. Your ability to provide justice is intrinsically tied in with your role as an adult. Remember that for most children, adults are still seen as the masters of the universe, the law-givers and the magistrates of all that is good and reasonable. Of course, this particular mask is, for many kids, cast off at an early age along with Santa Claus, but for most it is still the paradigm. Adults are supposed to be fair. Around the same time they realize that this isn't the case, the next thought they then have is 'Life's not fair', and so the spiral continues.

It is an act of appalling betrayal for an adult to be unfair to a child, precisely because it is an attribute so valued by society that we need to encourage it as much as possible; sure, we can never remedy the intrinsic unfairness of the world, but that's the point – we create communities for mutual benefit, not merely egoism. And if you want a child to grow up fair, he has to be treated fairly, otherwise he thinks, 'Oh well, sauce for the goose....'

How is justice conveyed in the classroom?

Scenario 1: I'm passing a classroom and I hear a commotion going on in the room next to me. I pop a head in and I see a year 7 pupil called

Roddy banging his hands on the desk in a way that suggests he is having a grand mal seizure; in fact, he is drumming his little heart out in a way that doesn't appear to match the learning objective on the board. The teacher is on the edge of freaking out. By all rights, he should be spending some time in the naughty bin. I take him out, and he runs away. Right, he's going higher up the ladder of consequence. Much more of this and I'll be sending for the child catcher and waxing off my iron maiden.

But when I finally get sat down with him, he tells me that the reason he's throwing a fit is because the teacher has been persistently threatening him with a phone call to his mum, who died three months ago. The teacher knows this, but keeps forgetting. To Roddy, this is the ultimate insult. Any hope she had of developing a relationship is being obliterated every time she opens her gob.

Now blind justice demands that Roddy does some time in the Big House for his crime, and normally I would back a teacher to the hilt and beyond (the handle?). But this is a kid on the edge, who's still dealing with grief. I have the right to have him excluded, but I don't. His behaviour is rotten, but we can perhaps understand it – without condoning it for a second, I might add – I've seen kids deal with traumas much worse with far more dignity. But there might be room for justice to be delivered through exception. So I put it to the teacher that the kid is having a hard time with his grief, and could she see his point of view? I ask her if she would apologize for her error – sincerely – to the kid, and set him a detention with her, in which she can have a chat and discuss ways forward. She agrees, and the damage if mended. And hopefully some good has been done.

Note that I'm not advocating simply making excuses for poor behaviour – God knows, education appears to be full of apologists who make excuses for children being essentially quite unpleasant. But even the law admits exceptions, crimes of passion, reduced responsibility and extenuating circumstances. It's why we have judges (however imperfect they may be) because we accept that, while justice needs to be blind to class, gender, privilege and wealth, there are always extenuating circumstances.

Scenario 2: A teacher (usually a new one, for reasons that will become clear) is trying to 'turn a class around' as the idiom has it (which makes it sound like you're slowly steering a large ship across the vast velvet turbulent blanket of the night sea. I mean, I get it, I get it, but the reality is more like pulling a spitfire out of a nosedive when you're just about to crash into the side of the Eiger at 500 miles an hour. I'm just saying. Turn it around, ha). The class, for reasons known, like the Unknown Soldier, only to God, are having none of it. 'Fuck your remedial pedagogy!' they shout, or something like that. There are so many acts of wilful disobedience and petty spite that it is difficult to see where misbehaviour ends and acts of neutrality begin. In short, it appears to be ALL of them at it. Although, crucially, she cannot be sure. What does justice demand?

One answer is to say that, to hell with the lot of them, keep the blasted lot of them in – the classic class detention. It has the elegant USP of simplicity. And that way, you're sure of catching the culprits. But the drawback is immense; you punish the innocent and the guilty alike, some kind of Old Testament extinction-level event, only this one will invariably not end in a rainbow. Result? You are HATED. Hated, and rightly so, by the (possibly minority) of the class who are genuinely trying to be less foul than the others. Raining on the just and the unjust alike simply proves that you are uninterested in justice, and more moved by retribution – in short, making yourself feel better. The wise teacher recognizes that this is a crucial test of justice, and a Rubicon for your relationship with the class.

These scenarios illustrate opposite extremes of the situation – too little justice is a reaving. But can you have too much justice? Aristotle hardly seemed to think so – the sole claim to viciousness lay in its deficiency. But I can imagine an excess, as in most things.

I now want to look at the virtues in more detail, and how they affect the teacher's lot.

6 Lion-Taming – Courage

"A ship is safe in harbor, but that's not what ships are for."

– *William Shedd*

Now we turn to courage, the virtue of appropriate bravery. What is bravery?

Bravery concerned Aristotle very much; he regarded it as being pivotal in a man's character. Under the name fortitude, the early Christian church defined it as one of the cardinal virtues. Why? Because it was the virtue from which all other virtues sprang. With this virtue, possessed in correct proportions, all other moral actions were possible; without it, they were not, as the agent would succumb to the vices of rashness or cowardice, and either avoid the straight path or pervert it. And I, Aristotle will no doubt be delighted to learn, agree. In teaching, as in life (which as a category embraces teaching, I believe – I'll do a Venn diagram later), courage is the quality that precedes all others. You can be a tyrant and teach (although I wouldn't advise it) but you cannot be a mouse. The question for any practitioner is; do you have the guts for the fight? Do you have the willpower to say to another human being, I know what is best for you? Courage is the root and the soil of authority. If you are fortunate to teach nothing but biddable Waltons, then even then you will need courage – the courage to push them to limits they themselves cannot dream of.

There is no job in which courage is not required. But I have never seen a job where it is so tested, so frequently, as those which involve dealing with the public. And dealing with the children of the public is just as demanding, if not more so. It is primarily a battle of wills, make no mistake. As I say, you may have very agreeable classes, but you are unlikely to have a class so blissfully helpful that you won't have to bend them to your will at some point. And it is more than likely that you will have to do it a lot.

Of course, this is not to say that you require the kind of courage that can face down the jaws of death – it isn't fearlessness that is required, and you will rarely be placed in physical danger, although it does happen. You are not a police officer, although some segments of the educational establishment may believe this to be true. Rather, it is a form of moral courage that is required; the courage to stand up for what you believe in, the courage to resist doing the wrong thing. You are, like it or not, a moral example to the children. Lady Gaga may not consider herself to be a role model, but you are – children learn by imitation, even the ugly ones. If they see that you have no dignity, self-restraint or manners, then they might feel that it isn't worth emulating you. You need to have the nerve to be the righteous man, yea, though your path may be beset on all sides by the inequities of the selfish and the tyrannies of evil men.

In Islam we have the concept of Jihad- the struggle to do the right thing. Unlike the popular Islamophobic stereotype, the idea of Jihad as a Holy War is what Muslims would call the lesser Jihad, the less important way to uphold the law of God. The Greater Jihad, the one that matters most, is the struggle to resist temptation in daily life, to stand up and be moral, even when the world is pushing you to do otherwise. This is the first form of courage that you, the teacher, will be required to have. Will you walk over to a bully in the playground, or will you walk away? Will you phone a parent, even though you know it'll be a thankless conversation if you're lucky? Will you apologize to a class if you lose their homework? In other words, have you got the stones to do what must be done?

I am not a brave man; I, like many people, suffer from a variety of fears, real and imagined. Several years ago, I was sent on a management training course in the middle of Wales, with a group of doomed, desperate people who were, like me, being groomed for middle-management greatness in the lower/middle end of the casual dining industry.

On one unhappy day, I found myself facing one of the most fearful moments of my life. I stood at the top of the Leap of Faith, a simple platform in the middle of the woods, perhaps a foot square, and only twenty or so feet from ground level. We all, each one of us, had to climb to the top, teeter on the edge, and to the whoops and calls of our supportive colleagues, face our fear and, you know, *do it anyway*. I watched the others with total indifference; heights mean little to me, beyond a natural aversion to actually falling from them.

But not this time; this time something odd happened as I contemplated the simple step forward into the air. The risks were non-existent, harnessed as I was into a truss that could have supported the weight of a small family car. That wasn't what I saw anyway. Something in the event had excavated a tiny childish trauma inside me – the memory, till that point forgotten, of climbing too high up a tree and being too scared to climb down again, like a child. I stayed up there, trapped by my anxiety for half an hour, until I could be coaxed down. That strange, buried bubble of frozen time resurfaced and burst as I stood at the platform; it was one of the oddest, most out-of-body experiences I can recall; seeing one thing, but feeling intuitively a whole suite of conflicting experiences. For a long time I stood there, feeling the colour drain away and the knowledge grow that I would not be able to do this simple thing. Below me, the encouragement had dissolved into a baying mockery, which had then reassembled into encouragement as they realized that I actually was on the edge of bottling out.

Then I stepped forward into space, my heart hammering away as though I was going to faint. They lowered me to the ground and I reassured everyone there that I was just messing with them. But I hadn't been. I had never been more terrified in my life, genuinely petrified with fright. When we returned to the conference base for a debrief and a session of sugar paper and felt-tip hell (I didn't realise that this was merely training for what passes as in-school training in my future life), I hid in my room and unexpectedly wept like an idiot for five minutes. Then, as quickly as it had blown up, the storm passed and I was completely fine again. The dark caverns of your emotions are strange places indeed. As I say, I am not brave. That step was harder than delivering a speech to a room full of dons. But at that point, I managed to tame the fear. At that point, I was brave. Rest assured, I have lived many other moments as an abject coward, in case you think I'm shining my shoes here.

This example shows us the different ways it is possible to perceive the concept of fear. Traditionally, argument about this quality has raged around the following point: is the truly brave man one who feels no fear, or the one who feels fear and still acts? The answer is more complicated than either extreme suggests.

For Aristotle, bravery was connected to reason; the brave man was one who experienced fear but had the faculty of putting it to one side in order to achieve his greater goals. In that respect, fear is an essential component of bravery: without the knowledge that one could be frightened there is no sense of overcoming the fear. Without the reason to acknowledge that the thing one faces is potentially destructive or undesirable, the sense that one understands what one is doing is lost. There is no bravery, for example, in walking along a broomstick blindfolded, unless you are aware that you are on the edge of a cliff (although why you should be doing so escapes me; perhaps Leatherface was in charge of your stag night).

Yet there is also the risk of over-analyzing your fears, of dwelling too much on them. Have you ever turned the lights out in a room and then hurried just a little bit because you don't want to get murdered? Have you ever seen a scary movie and then avoided the dark short cut on the way home? Ever checked your back seat twice because you were thinking about an urban myth? Most people have, even as they curse their stupidity for doing so, like saluting a magpie or avoiding a ladder. Or perhaps you've been called to speak in public, and worked yourself into an anxious jelly by imagining the worst, and how unfunny you actually are. This has never happened to me, of course.

So, while reason and bravery are intimately connected, there are extremes of excess and deficiency in both respects. The brave man or woman is aware of the dangers they face, but then doesn't think too deeply about them so as to avoid being paralyzed by them. Another factor that Aristotle would have us consider is that bravery is enormously subjective – we must all work out our own appropriate responses to different situations and context, and then adjust our bravery levels accordingly.

Example: As a teacher, you meet people all the time, and a new kid in the room is hardly a cause for much concern. However, you've been told that you will be the proud midwife to the first day of a child who has been excluded from several schools prior to yours, on the grounds that he walks up to teachers he doesn't like and punches them 'in the charlies'. You know that today is likely to be interesting. You may even perceive a higher level of threat. You may put a textbook down the front of your long johns, just in case.

So why is this virtue such a big deal in schools, and for teachers? Because the job is, or can be, extremely intimidating. There are an enormous number of situations where you will be called upon to man up or mouse out. Bravery, at least in an educational context, can be required in a number of ways. For example, many NQTs or trainee teachers I know seem to be paralyzed with anxiety but enthusiastic to get started in equal measures. The level of fear they often experience is unlike the first-day nerves of most other professions, bar deep-sea oil mining or bomb disposal. To the inexperienced teacher, the unexperienced classroom is home to all manner of faceless perils. They say that the scariest thing in cinema and story is what you can't see, as evidenced by such horror teases as *Psycho*, *The Blair Witch Project*, *Paranormal Activity* and *The Omen*.[1] There is nothing scarier than a bump in the night when you're alone in the house. This is the dilemma a new class presents to us, especially when *we* are new.

Even if we are not, the conventional demands of the profession routinely expect us to face that which we might fear – a room full of people whom we will ask to perform tasks that they are unlikely to want to carry out being the chief one. Is hell other people, as Sartre suggests? Perhaps not, but they provide the potential for existential horror unequalled anywhere else. Is there anything more terrible than being ignored? Is there a greater dissolution of the self than having an entire room full of people explicitly pretend that you are neither visible nor audible. 'Can anyone hear anything?' That sort of thing. This is one of the greatest fears of the teacher.

There are other fears too: the fear of being made to look a fool, of kids being rude, personal and arrogant, and you being unable to do a thing about it. This is the kind of stress that, unchecked, leads teachers to look at hammers and imagine what they could do with one.[2] Unless you have experienced this, it's hard to imagine how humiliating it is – and that is the absolutely correct word for it – to have a child, less than half your age, swear at you with a smile, or call you useless, or wonder loudly when the real teacher is coming? That, coupled with the fact that actually spannering them is rather frowned on these days.

Other fears, more remote, but still real enough to depress us, are the headline-grabbers: the assaults, the sexual harassment, the bullying and savagery, the chair-chucking that unfortunately will always afflict those of us who choose to work with large, unfiltered sectors of the public. I have been pushed up against a wall by a student, threatened with a stick, sworn at on numerous occasions, and experienced more personal, in-your-face violence in the classroom than I ever did in eight years running nightclubs in the Wild, Wild West of Soho; I absolutely mean that. Part of it is the problem that some children don't see playground threats and violence as serious; acts that would have you before a magistrate in the outside world get treated as a 'school matter' within the walls of a comprehensive. Unfortunately many senior management (and even teachers) often collude with this. Of course, they are exactly as serious, and just

---

[1] And not by torture-porn car crashes like *Saw* and *Hostel*, where fear is replaced by the revulsion against viscera

[2] Sir Ken Robinson would no doubt applaud the ingenuity.

as upsetting, and just as terrifying. Of course, such incidents are rare, but then so are plane crashes and shark attacks, and extreme spectrum events have a habit of dominating our imaginations in a way that reassuring statistics do not.

There are other fears, more gentle ones: the fear that a student will underachieve; the fear that you will be deemed unsatisfactory in a formal observation; the fear that you will never see your friends again due to the mountain of marking facing you. The fear that you will never conquer the mountain of marking due to the enormous number of friends you have with glasses of wine. There are innumerable fears. We work in an intensely social environment; our job is people. And people are often very scary indeed.

But there are other fears that are stitched more closely into the job experienced, not the job described (in ads, usually). When a pupil is unsubtly tapping what is undoubtedly a moronic cussing text to their sub-literate chum under the desk, you have a different kind of fear; the fear of having to do something. You might look at the little lovely and think to yourself, 'That's against the rules – I know that. But I also know that if I mention it, I have to confiscate it. And that's going to mean a stand-up row. The class are working so well. It seems a shame to disturb them.' You look around, and a little part of you dies inside. 'I'll just ignore it,' you say to yourself.

Sound familiar? We've all done it. In fact, I'd say that this is the routine experience of many teachers' days: tacitly ignoring bad behavior because it will lead to high levels of inconvenience. What's at stake here is a kind of fear – the fear that, if we step up to the students and actually challenge them on what we can see them doing, they'll call us on it. 'Or else?' is one of the scariest things we can hear as teachers. And inside you can hear yourself saying, 'He's right. What *do* I do about it?' Far easier – and less courageous – simply to ignore it; to walk past the girls hooting like geese on the stairs outside the class sitting an exam; to walk past the groups of boys listening to mobiles inside the school; to ignore the uniform hanging off them like rags; to ignore the scores of pupils who are doing far, far too little in class, but just enough to appear to be sitting, facing the right way and holding a pen quietly. It takes courage to step up to these people and make an issue of it. It really does.

But this is something that we as teachers have to do on a routine basis. That word *routine* is appropriate here, because the good news is that the more we exercise out authority in this manner, gradually the less we have to exercise it, with children who know us, at least. Aristotle believed that the best way to improve virtues of character was to practise them. When I started teaching, even though I had a boisterous, social career behind me, it still turned my guts to ice to think about facing a group of teenagers and talking to them about cultures and customs of our world neighbours. You may find that hard to believe. But the more you do it, the easier it gets, until a few years down the line you're practically wondering what the big fuss was about in the first pace.

Of course, many teachers get over this first, initial foundational fear of stepping into a classroom. They learn that with repetition, like all sensations, it gets dulled. As any whisky drinker will tell you, it's an acquired taste. But the mistake they then make is to allow themselves to develop just enough courage to turn up and deliver a lesson, but not enough courage to get really stuck into the class. It's as if they've decided that they'll take a few bruises so that they can stay in the classroom and survive but, like the kid holding the pen but not doing anything, they'll never develop a strong relationship with the class; they'll never drive them to learn beyond their own inclinations; and they'll probably teach the same lesson for the next twenty years.

Going from humble to assertive

But if you want to really flourish as a teacher, you'll have to learn to acknowledge that a lot of what you want to do will require some high-wire work, like the men who built the skyscrapers. You will have to do a lot more than turn up, drop the lesson off like a turd and leave when the bell rings. Just holding on in between the start and the finish. You'll need to *demand* good behaviour; to follow up on that behaviour when required; to call students out constantly for underachieving; to push them even when they don't want to be pushed; to insist that homework gets done; to remind them when they're disappointing you; to tell them when what they've done is rubbish, instead of constantly praising everything they do as if they were tiny Caligulas.

I have rarely seen a career where, to be successful, you have to display courage so constantly. This is because your entire career involves not just standing in a room and talking about geography or William Shakespeare, but in bending others to your will; to showing them that you have something valuable for them to learn, and that if they won't do it the way you've asked then by Jim they'll swing for it. You will constantly be clashing personality against personality, and exercising authority in a room full of people who may be indisposed to accord it to you.

The good news is that, as with all other virtues of character, this is slowly acquired through experience and repetition, which means inuring yourself to the challenges of the things that cause you fear. Scared of them ignoring you when you ask them to pipe down? Ask them to pipe down, and then do something about the ones who don't. And then do it again. And again. Eventually, if you're fair (see: *justice*) and consistent, all but the very belligerent will begin to acquiesce with your demands (and for them you can devise all kinds of personal 'behaviour strategies'). The pay-off from this is that the more you do it, the easier it becomes for you to do it … and better still, the less you'll need to display the virtue in the first place because the class will behave more and more for you, and require you to be brave less and less.

Eventually you get to the point where it isn't a question of being brave in the classroom any more – it's simply not a concern. You will still be aware of the risks of bad behaviour (because your reason tells you that such things can still happen, no matter how good the relationship is) but know that the risk is unlikely. And then you'll be more worried about other virtues, and at least you're not simply worried about getting them to follow you all the time.

Bravery is one of the key virtues to teaching, for the reasons I've described. The biggest vice lies in its deficiency; cowardice from the teacher is fatal to the education in the classroom. When I started teaching, although I would never had admitted it, I was a moral coward. I would rail and rant at poor behaviour (I had no fear of doing that, so I thought that I was a brave man) but I was subconsciously scared that if I set detentions or did anything other than blow a gale at the whole class, then I would be ignored, or that nothing would come of it, or that I would look like a bad teacher. So I never set any detentions, or did anything other than practically perish with the exasperation of trying to run classrooms through force of will. Courage take many forms; just because you're not physically scared of them (as I wasn't) doesn't mean that you're not petrified by their scorn, or their ignorance.

Perseverance: the courage to keep going

Then there is the courage required simply to turn up. How many teachers have begged off from school, or put off lesson-planning until the last, the very last minute, because it's 'that class'. I think every teacher who has ever taught in mainstream education will appreciate what I mean; every class has its own dynamic, and every class has a different dynamic with every different teacher. How often have you heard another teacher say (annoyingly), 'Well, they behave fine for me.' Or, '9J? Oh, I love that class. Sure, they're a bit sparky, but you can really get great discussion going with them.' If there were a God in heaven who cared about such things, you would be legally permitted to pie such people.

Sometimes it takes resolve simply to walk into the same room as the 'special' class. For me, it was my short course GCSE students, who had been specially selected for the bottom set, and knew all about it. They also knew that I was fresh from the packet, and had all the authority of a bowl of custard. I dreaded going into that class; eventually, I simply stopped planning meaningful lessons for them, simply because so few of them even tried to do what I asked them to do. They sat in the right seats, and that was about all. Some of them openly called me names, and when I asked them to move seats, they would literally look at me and laugh. The night before I taught them, I would feel a pit develop in my stomach, and my whole evening would be ruined in the anticipation of the humiliation and drubbing I would receive at their hands.

With such classes, some teachers develop a bunker mentality – just walk in, survive, and get the hell out. I certainly did. That alone takes a small level of courage. Taking it to the next step, of course, requires a deeper, more textured courage.

Bravery also means doing the right thing in the face of shame or disapproval. In teaching, this can take many forms. In the classroom, it can be easy to give in to the demands of the children, simply because that's the way the stream's flowing and where it's going doesn't seem so bad after all. It's the last day of term, and the class walks in, one by one, as if primed, all saying the same thing. 'Are we doing any work today?' Or, 'Can we have a fun lesson?' Where do they learn this phrase? Is there a memo they all get at some point? Given the ubiquity of social networking, I imagine it would be quite easy. But children, like hives of bees or stacks of ants, have a colony mind, and know that with persistence and repetition many great trees can be felled. You might very well have planned a lovely revision session; you might very well have thought to treat your class by giving them ten minutes to chat at the end of a hard term. But how easy it seems simply to look at them all looking at you, with those mournful, expectant eyes, and think, 'Oh, why not?' Out comes the DVD of *Big Momma's House 7*, and everyone's happy.

Except that 'being happy' isn't the aim of your game. The objective is a good education, and if every kid expects (and gets) jelly and ice cream for the last day of term, then why the hell is school open at all? Might as well close for that day. Which then makes Thursday the NEW last day, and the whole process continues. No, no matter how hard they howl, you have to stand your ground. If YOU want to give them a 'reward lesson' (but aren't they all?) then so be it, but the key is not to let them tell you to do so. Don't imagine that you're being democratic and inclusive by doing so – you're not: you're letting them tell you how to run your room. And it is your room.

That's the guiding principle that constitutes the kernel of your authority: this is your space. My room, my rules. This isn't to say that you run it like an autocratic tyrant – the focus, the goal of your rule needs to be their educational wellbeing. The teacher who demonstrates high levels of control simply because they want to enjoy the exercise of power, or feel the fruits of dominance, shouldn't be allowed to take a class. But your room it is, to run as best fits the lesson. They sit where *you* want. They follow your – reasonable – instructions. This all requires spine; not so much that you drown them in dominance, but enough that they know someone is in charge, and that someone is looking after them.

The courage to defy the desires of others

This is the key. As children, we progress to adulthood in a continual pursuit of autonomy and liberty; this, as J. S. Mill pointed out, was the human condition. The natural history of man is the history of emancipation. This parallel also applies to the growth of the individual, not just human culture through the centuries. Inevitably, children initially accept the demands that adults place upon them; they simply know no other condition. As they grow, they realize that they have ambitions and desires contrary to or at least concurrent with those of their parents; the battle for independence begins, and parents wonder where they went wrong for the next twenty years or so.

As children enter the adolescent phase, they start to perceive themselves as something other than simply extensions of their parents; they start to reflect on what it means to be themselves; they form an identity. This is the difficult bit. The easiest way that we can understand who we are is by defining who we are not. How much easier it is than establishing what our core values are. It is easier to say what we hate than what we love. So, for a while at least, many teenagers progress through a phase of rejecting many things that they previously took for granted. This negativity is commonly associated with the surly, sulky teenager. As we get older still, hopefully we enter a phase where we start to find things that matter to us: we attach meaning and value to abstracts that we feel constitute meaningful parts of our personality and character. We define ourselves.

And while this happy process is proceeding, you're trying to teach them. Free from the privations of the parental sphere, many students find that the school environment, so heavily dominated as it is by people the same age and height as themselves, acts as a microcosm of the real world. They flex their emergent personalities and muscles, and often try to get away with as much as humanly possible. We are in love with liberty, or at least our perception of it. The most common definition of freedom is that of negative freedom: freedom from restraint; we rage and howl against any attempt to distract or detain us from our desires. And this, I'm afraid, is where we come in.

Putting twenty-five children in one room and asking them to differentiate equations, is the very definition of thwarting their natural desire for freedom. Who can blame them? This is a perfectly natural state. Even adults find it hard to cope with a loss of their freedom – being stuck in a traffic jam, behind a slow walker, or simply waiting in line on a call hold queue proves that we are no strangers to resentment. But this is an enormous part of the job. For those who claim that education should always be fun, and that this is the way to guarantee that pupils are motivated, I say good luck to you. Education is not always fun. It should always be valuable, in some way, however you define it, But it will not always be as much fun as say, updating your status on Facebook, or playing *Call of Duty* on the PS3. It just can't be, not all the time. I try to make my lessons interesting, but ultimately I cannot make something inter-esting for everyone. I love my subject, but part of learning about it, for me, involved learning facts, memorizing details, and hard, hard work over books. That's the legwork required to learn anything. This simply will not be denied. If you think that you can educate in a continual process of excitement and joy, then you clearly have access to faculties denied to the rest of us. Or perhaps you're just a bit mental.

In a classroom, your job is to bend others to your will. Your will should be aimed at their education, but bending them is something you will have to do. Few students are so amenable as to be a hundred per cent co-operative under all circumstances. It is likely that your classes will be populated not by slavish automatons, but by auton-omous individuals, with ideas of their own about how things should be run. This is where courage is required most, and most consistently in teaching. You need to stand up to others in the classroom, and defy them when they attempt, quite naturally, to return the pressure back to you. This pressure can take the form of begging, wheedling, defiance, negotiating, intimidation and many other behaviours, but it is all to one purpose – the dominance of the room. The dominance should be yours. Rule the room, and do so with courage.

The courage to be a professional

There is also the courage required to be a professional in other contexts. As a professional, you will have your own ideas about the correct way, or at least the most efficient way, to teach. Many teachers feel swamped by a deluge of best practice, advice and requirements from senior staff, line managers, local educational authorities, teacher trainers and so on. It would appear that there are as many opinions about how you should best teach as there are people with voices to express an opinion. It took me a few years to understand that most of this body of opinion is exactly that – just an opinion. Eventually you may find yourself rebelling against the requirements upon you. You may question the latest initiative as ideological, well-meant but preposterous.

For example, by the time I entered the profession I was told with perfect seriousness that no teacher should mark with a red pen; shades more arboreal were required. The reason was – so it went – that red had connotations of negativity, disapproval, and students found it demotivating. Whereas green was, I imagine, the colour of champions, reflection, and cool, considered formative learning.

This is, I might point out, a complete load of sh*t.

I have searched and searched and searched for the origin of this fantasy, and have so far come up with no research that seriously supports this proposition. Of course, there has been an enormous amount of psychological research that suggest many colours have certain emotional and cultural associations attached to them. But this is far, far from suggesting that students simply switch off from cherry but switch on to emerald. Part of the 'research' that suggested this was so was based on respondent surveys. Typically students would be asked, 'How do you feel when you see your homework returned covered in red ink?' Rare was the student who didn't say, 'A bit rubbish.' Of course they did. They were getting feedback that was (usually) indicative of what they could have done better. Who really likes being told that their work was flawed? Any colour would have conveyed that impression.

The point is that you will be subject to endless direction by perfectly well-meaning people who have nothing but the best intentions in their hearts and apparently marbles inside their heads. This would be fine if you weren't doing something so vital, so impossibly important as educating children; but you are. And that means that your concern must always be the educational wellbeing of the child. You're not simply a drone on a conveyer belt – you're a professional, and that implies an enormous amount of responsibility. If we want respect, we have to act as though we deserve it. I'm not just talking about unionism here (although it could also be part of this project). I'm talking about conducting ourselves and our teaching as if it were the project of a trained professional, and not treating ourselves as childminders for hire.

If you have a professional opinion, discuss it; if you object to what you're being told, raise it. Of course, we all act as agents within a hierarchy – unless you happen to own the school, and pay everyone's wages, you need to acknowledge that you play a part in a greater whole. But this doesn't mean that you need to accept brainlessly everything that is passed your way. You have a brain, a professional qualification, and a responsibility to others that surpasses mere slavish adherence to the rules. Would that be your defence before St Peter at the Pearly Gates? I was doing my job?

The courage to deal with parents

Professional courage also extends into other realms: for instance, the parental one. Parents have their own concerns, of course, and don't occupy the fabulous world of glamour and mystery that we teachers do. They usually don't speak and think in the same way that educational professionals do. Never forget that in all but the most exceptional circumstances, they have a far greater concern for the child's wellbeing than you do (I say this because I am repeatedly horrified to hear teachers speak to parents as if they were some kind of inconvenience to their job, and that if they could only shut the hell up, everyone would be happier). Parents are, can be, need to be, allies in the teaching project. If they support you, then the child is supported and you have the strength of ten. If they defy you, you'll be putting out bushfires in your classroom until graduation day.

They are important allies. I nearly said 'stakeholders' there, but then I'd have to kill myself for shame. They're not stakeholders, and neither are you: you're parents and teachers. Those are the roles; those are the best definitions that language and social evolution have provided for us. Raising and teaching a child isn't equivalent to placing a bet on a dog.

You need to be in contact with some, maybe many of them. But the process is a diplomatic one, and often an area where the teacher loses his or her nerve in the gap between classroom and home. A phone call terrifies many teachers. You can hear it in their voices; they call up, and launch into a rant against the child and the parent without a breath. They do this because they're terrified of being interrupted, and don't allow the parent to speak. You might as well send a letter or leave a message on an answering machine. Be brave enough to greet them with civility, and ask them if this is a convenient time to speak. Say something nice about the child (which I can recommend as being one of the simplest and most effective tactics any teacher can use – the parent sees the best in their child, and by showing that you can see it too – even if it is very, very faint – then you put yourself on a footing of agreement and consensus before you've even tackled the reason for the call.)

But always say what needs to be said; don't shy away from the topic; be clear, be calm, be direct, and have the guts to say what you wanted to say. I find it helps to write down the key points I need to get across on a piece of paper in front of me as we speak so that I don't forget in the noise of the conversation. Props like that can immeasurably aid your confidence and ultimately your courage. But you need the steel actually to make the call, in exactly the same way you need to steel yourself for some classes; with patience and practice it becomes easier, but initially it's the least used tactic of many newer teachers. More experienced teachers too, if they haven't got into the habit of it.

One of the bravest things I have ever heard is the story of Hugh Thomson, the hero, if ever there was one, of the My Lai massacre. A helicopter pilot during the Vietnam War, he put his chopper in between a group of Vietnamese civilians and a platoon of American soldiers intent on murdering them; he even ordered his crew to fire upon his fellow Americans if they didn't stand down. Villified by the army, it took decades for his heroism to be recognized.

Maximillian Kolbe was a Polish Catholic Priest, imprisoned in Auschwitz during World War II. Seeing one of his fellow prisoners being taken away to be executed, he volunteered to take his place instead, even though the man was a stranger to him. Later, being starved to death by his captors, he led his fellow prisoners in prayer, and even offered his arm to receive a lethal injection of acid at the very end.

Both of these stories, although exemplifying extremes of courage under duress, illustrate a simple point: bravery is not a function of great skill, intelligence or ability; it is simply choosing to act in a brave way, despite the pressure to do otherwise. In other words, it is available to us all, like some impossibly valuable resource inside everyone. We simply choose to possess it. Or, more often, not.

7   I am Waiting – Patience

Patience, far from being the mousy virtue of the librarian, is closely linked to courage. It describes fortitude under pressure, and the ability to bear intolerable loads with tolerance and calm. It sounds, to be fair, the dreariest of qualities, with its associations with high levels of boredom, and a seeming inability to produce and provoke action and passion. Nietzsche said that patience was the least valuable of human qualities, because it offended the proper sense of animation and life that existing required. I suspect Nietzsche was a barrel of laughs in a doctor's waiting room. It would be entertaining watching him try to call IT support for a laptop and seeing how he fared.

The best thing to do

As a culture, we are obsessed with action; inactivity is seen as intrinsically slothful and sinful. To be fair, it often is, and the term 'couch potato' isn't pejorative because we're offended by vegetables or furniture. I have (because I am friendless) a favourite logical syllogism which I'll quote. It's taken from a British political, satirical sitcom called 'Yes Minister', which by modern standards appears to be the very last word in political probity. In it, the mercurial civil servant, Sir Humphrey Appleby, is lecturing the minister Jim Hacker about the reason why, at all costs, politicians must be seen to be decisive and active:

> *Premise one:* We must do something
> *Premise two:* This is something
> *Conclusion:* Therefore we must do this.

You can see the logic operating behind this piece of inanity. Whenever an offence to public order is committed, the next step after trauma inevitably seems to be the demand that *something* must be done, and fast. In the aftermath of every gunshot tragedy, calls to pass restrictive laws are almost as immediate as the sound of the shot. The death of a child in care creates a tsunami of political will to transform the culture of social services. In the case of the death of Victoria Climbie, jobs were lost, fingers were pointed, and a whole raft of policies were implemented in the fervent desire to show that something was, indeed, being done. Despite the fact that such events are horribly routine, the urgency that was displayed by the public and the public servants who serviced them was enormous. Something must be done. Something must always be done.

But must it? In almost every meeting to discuss any matter, how often do we consider the option that dare not speak its name – do nothing? Who would be bold enough to present inactivity as the right thing to do, the best way to proceed? Who would have the heart (there's courage again) to address a press conference, or a PTA meeting, or any crowd clamouring for direction, and tell them with confidence and pride that you had decided to do nothing? And yet this is often exactly what should be done in a huge number of situations. Consider the chef, seasoning a pot of stew; he has decided that it has reached optimal saltiness or heat. So what then should he do if the commis chef asks, what do we do with it now, boss? Tell him to whack another peck of pepper in? Of course not. It's ready – it doesn't need anything else. If a painter is satisfied that he's mixed just the right shade of vermilion for the night canvas he's preparing, does he add a blob of scarlet to see if he can go one better?

Patience is famously a virtue. But beyond that rather mealy-mouthed aphorism, what is it? Taking Aristotle's recommendation, it is the mid-point between two vicious extremes: the excess of over-tolerance, and the deficiency of rashness.

Patience as the ability to defer gratification

There is nothing else for it: life is not a bed or roses, nor is it a box of chocolates (except inasmuch as you frequently find yourself choking on a strawberry cream or a despicable ginger rather than the Elysian jackpots of Turkish delight or caramels, despite their completely identical appearances and the mocking uncertainties of the map, which is invariably either hand drawn – which appears incredible in this virtual age – or integrated into the underside of the box, thereby reducing the simple act of chocolate identification to a graceless balancing act that often ends in a rain of confectionary and a churlish grab at the first three that hit the carpet. But I digress). This acknowledgement of a truth universally observed has an obvious point that apparently eludes some: we can't always get what we want.[1]

Before I drown in platitudes and song titles, I must point out that it would seem that surely nobody thinks that life really *is* easy, do they? Well, perhaps not consciously, but many seem to operate on the axiom that the world should apparently bend over backwards to kiss them on the back cheeks. The psychologist Lawrence Kohlberg would call this the Self-Interested Stage of moral development, the toddler state where the very young view the world as an enormous playground and an extension of their desires. After all, to many children it would appear that everything, in a curiously infantile version of the Anthropic Principle, is created with one thing in mind; the satisfaction of their whims. Every baby is a Caligula and a Napoleon rolled into one. Do not for a second imagine that children are born purely altruistic, and that they would hesitate for even a fraction of a heartbeat to see you utterly annihilated in an instant if it brought their rusk or rattle a metre closer to their ravenous, *a posteriori* maw. They might regret your absence – but out of egoism, not out of altruism. Believe me.

This state is natural; the child develops a sense of self, then a sense of other, and then, in the manner of every good empiricist, builds up a picture of the world idea by idea. Noticing that others exist is one of the first things. After that, at some nebulous point in the future, comes caring about those other people.

Some people seem never to reach this stage; they trip along, or rather, barrel along in the manner of a pinball, from situation to situation, crashing into everything and expecting others to clean up; they act as though everyone else was merely a bit-part player in the enormous self-penned melodrama of their lives, and that they exist only by their whim, in the manner of Vishnu – as soon as they awake, the whole world vanishes like a dream. And most importantly, they lack the ability to deny themselves whatever crosses their tiny mind at the time, and meet any obstacle to their fancies with gusts and gales of protest, upset at the natural order of things. In other words, they cannot self-defer.

This capacity to restrain oneself is no mere adornment to personality; it has been identified as one of the most fundamental attributes

---

[1] As Mick Jagger famously pointed out. Although for a man who can allegedly pull £190 million from the back of his sofa, this seems a strange restriction to describe.

necessary for success, which although is a nebulous concept itself, can be defined at least in these terms: the ability to forgo some temporary, lesser gain in order to secure a greater one. It is the farmer who waits until the crops are ripe before he harvests them; the boxer who waits until he's in top condition before he puts himself into the ring; the F1 driver who sits in the back four, denying himself an early, easy way forward, until the perfect line appears and he drives clear of the pole-man.

Patience. Few things that we value can be gained in an instant. Low fruit are picked first, but lack flavour. Every man must plan to achieve anything worth having: a relationship; a career; a skill; a degree; a well-built house; a garden; a business. Unless you plan to live life by persistently winning at scratch cards or inheriting wealth you need to be able to say 'no' to a life of immediate ease, and 'yes' to waiting for opportunity to present itself.

Many children in schools clearly have no idea of this. Part of the problem is, of course, their lack of temporal reference. When I was 16, I went to university to study Electrical Engineering: I was precocious, and easily swayed by a persuasive Physics teacher who convinced me that there might be some money in it. Two days later, I realized that a life of mathematics and code, while lucrative – and easy enough – filled me with existential dread. I realized in a heartbeat that I was Humanities to the core, and science would only ever be my mistress; so I returned to school, to finish off upper sixth. At the time I thought my life was over. Can you imagine it? I would be SEVENTEEN by the time I finally started university! Nearly dead!

I smile now, but at the time I thought that the delay was a disaster. To a child, a week is a long time, and a year is unimaginable. Observe the large numbers of students who don't start taking their GCSE exams seriously until they loom large enough for the distance to be counted in weeks, on their hands. Perspective of time is vital to this sense of deferred gratification, when an hour is a light year away. 'Five more minutes' is the refrain that every teenager placates (or attempts to placate) their parents with a morning arousal, convinced that three hundred seconds will be enough time to fall asleep and wake up, fresh as a lazy daisy.

The virtue of the man who endures: fortitude as patience

Patience is first applauded in the Western tradition by the Christian Church. Given its broadly dualistic approach to existence – the material world playing second fiddle to the world of spirit, thought and soul – Christians have been encouraged since the Acts of the Apostles to see the ability to wait and endure as a crucial human quality. This world, it need scarcely be said, is a vale of tears to many, and it raineth on the just and the unjust alike and bugger me, doesn't it though?

It occurred to me as recently as my mid-twenties that life was, essentially, mostly troublesome. It has been estimated that were all the matter in the universe to be compressed into a cube, it would take up a neat and tidy 0.000000000000000028 per cent of the volume of the known universe. There is, it must be said, a lot of nothing punctuated by a very tiny scattering of something. In its own way, life is like this; enormous long stretches of boredom, discomfort and disappointment, desperation and anxiety.

Consider any average day in your own life, and I can practically guarantee that the vast majority of it would be mercilessly edited out of the biopic they will eventually make about you to reward you for services to humanity. We can barely imagine Gandhis and Einsteins and Lincolns scratching their famous asses or picking walnuts from their teeth. But these are the mainstays of all of our lives – and that's in countries of relative affluence and ease, in a century where many of the discomforts and inconveniences of our ancestors have been dispelled. To paraphrase Thomas Hobbes, life for many in the world, for most of the time, is nasty, brutish and short. One can imagine the attraction of the promises of Christianity in a world that did indeed seem to be soiled, sad and painful.

And yet … there has to be a reason to endure the river of shit that rains and rains down upon us constantly, and so there is. Few things of value are easily obtained; indeed, it might truthfully be said that the difficulty in their procurement is proportionate to the value we place on them. Love, position, precious moments, the velocity and location of one's life at any instant – all are framed and magnified by the trials it takes to unearth them. Satisfaction is fleeting; we are never content for more than a moment, and as soon as one satisfaction is obtained, a new and wider goal replaces it as the next summit to scale. Patience is the path that takes us from one point to the next, that makes endurance possible. Its absence leads to the vice – naturally – of impatience, and an inability to allow one's palate to be cleansed ready for the next moment of value. Unprepared, we become unable to recognize such moments when they occur, and we spiral into a vortex of faster and faster gratification, the terminus of which is moronic sensuality and nihilism.

This is one of the tricks of teaching: to be the patient man, to learn to endure, but in a meaningful way. The idiot teacher wants to see results in a day, and miracles in a week. This is, some might say (e.g. me) the way that continuous assessment has been embedded in contemporary teaching – in an ideal observation lesson (and I use the term 'ideal' with the irony I would normally reserve for phrases like 'a tasty shit sandwich'), where the teacher, in order to display their mad skills to the dispassionate observer, needs to show that progress has been demonstrably achieved in the space of fifty minutes. Results, Smiggins, results, and damn the idea that education might not be so easily charted in convenient fifty-minute nuggets, like sausages being nipped efficiently as they get squeezed out of some mechanical cloaca. Worse, schools now have to show that results improve year on year, as if education, like the expansion of a successful company manufacturing paper clips or the progress of a mould on a Petri dish, was subject to the law of infinite expansion. Which is fabulous – by the year 2032 I expect to see 155 per cent of my children exceeding the maximum possible targets for their GCSEs, and all of my children being above average.

God, give me Strength.

There is little, room, it seems, for patience in the contemporary classroom and school. Nor is this rot exclusive to the local level – this stems directly from the ministerial level, where targets must be met to justify careers and policies; where the average tenure of the average government minister – and they are VERY average, to be fair – is less than fourteen months, and any trick they try has to show flower and fruit long before they have to pack their bags and move into the Ministry for Jelly Babies or something. Patience has been ejected from the list of contemporary virtues, as unsuitable for the demands of a demanding age.

Well fine, but that's tough titty for the age, because the role of the teacher demands it. Why? Because students, being human, don't always show linear progress. Which is odd, because we evaluate them as if their intellectual attainment were in some way proportionate to their height. But as anyone who has ever tested a child twice over any period can testify, since children don't necessarily get smarter or more stupid over the course of a day or so, their progress can't be so quickly measured. This is because understanding, like most abstract processes, doesn't follow the straight line of graph paper: small mental breakthroughs happen in fits and starts; eureka moments occur in the unlikeliest of environments; effort varies from child to child and from day to day, so that children who have been working at straight Ds all year can suddenly put in a fit of effort towards their exams and leap up to a B.

The patience to build relationships

It takes a new teacher a long, long time to build up relationships with his class – maybe a year, maybe more or less, depending on the demographic, the rigour of the school, the teacher, and a million other factors. How often have I heard a teacher wail at me, 'I tried the things you advised; detentions, praise, clear boundaries, and they're still acting up.' The teacher is usually talking to me after a few weeks of these methods, oblivious to the fact that such strategies can take months and months and months of time. But they have been trained to expect results that happen as swiftly as sodium dropped into water, buzzes and bubbles. The human character is far less prescribed than that.

Patience in excess – the vice

Nietzsche disagreed; he saw it as the barrier to passion: 'passion will not wait.' And perhaps the old syphilitic bounder had a point. After all, there is another vice associated with patience, the vice of excess, or impassivity – to bear too much, to endure situations that require action, and to be sure this is a situation we often see in teaching, when a teacher has developed an insensitivity to the poor behaviour in his classroom, on the grounds that 'it's just like that' and nothing is to be done; or has begun to assume that vicious name-calling is part and parcel of teaching certain sets of teenagers, or to expect low grades from children because they come from 'that' sort of a background. There are some things that should not be endured, that shouldn't be stood for, even if doing so appears to be the answer to some immediate problem. It is often, it is true, easier to allow children's ambitions to sag below the horizon than it is to keep pushing them to exceed themselves.

As with all the virtues, excess and deficiency are to be abhorred; patiently waiting to be defeated, patiently watching a child being bullied, patiently enduring insults and torment are not examples where patience is a sign of the flourishing teacher. Rather, it is a sign of the teacher who has lost the spirit for the fight. And it demands action, not inaction. As ever, the balance must be found. It is rarely easy.

Nietzsche felt that patience was intrinsically self-defeating – literally, in that it acted on the virtuous man as an obstacle to action, and allowed him to tolerate intolerable levels of coercion and restriction from others, weaker than himself. The notion of the Superman is found in this idea, the unbound Prometheus who resists all attempts at restriction by the weak and the mean-spirited. Life is for those who seize it. We don't have to adopt the whole nine yards of Nietzsche's attempts to defend the indefensible position that the weak should be tyrannized by the strong in order to see that impassivity undermines the root of the role of the teacher – to act, to participate, to guide, to train, to protect. Standing by and doing nothing doesn't fit well with this role.

Endurance in the classroom

'The virtue of patience is that habit by which we endure hardship so that we maintain the course of action set out by reason.'[2]

But there are benefits to adopting the manner of patience: in a classroom where behavior is commonly unsettled, the teacher is often faced with the temptation to try to fix each and every situation that breaks the rules of the room. A noble aim, but often with an unfortunate end – the teacher becomes swamped with a tsunami of low level disruptions that steal all his time away and leave him with handfuls of ashes, and no lesson. Far better that the teacher tacitly endures some of the lower problems – and I mean strategically endure, not just ignore – in order to tackle some of the more pressing issues, the actions of the dangerous or outrageous. Pen-clickers and toe-tappers can wait until the big fish have been fried. This type of endurance is very hard to pull off; many of us are so primed for any event of impropriety that we cannot bear to see it occur, and feel that instant action is demanded. Sometimes we have to endure this kind of behaviour in order to achieve what we really want.

Patience and faith

Then there's patience linked to something I can only describe as faith, and to hell with the sensitivities of Dawkins et al. Actually, though, this is the faith that everyone shares, whether Jew, Hindu, Mormon or

---

2   www.catholiceducation.org/articles/education/ed0283.html

Humanist: the faith that something is possible, or can happen, even if the evidence isn't … well, let's say ISN'T THERE yet. A student whom you know – but only intuitively, and certainly nothing you can quantify in a demonstrable way – is capable of passing a subject, or reaching a grade, or mastering a concept or an instrument or even a word, but you couldn't prove it to anyone else. This aspect of knowledge – the unproven fact, or knowledge of the unknowable – is most commonly identified with the *a priori* belief system of mystics and theologians, but is absolutely fundamental to the way that all of us, rationalists, empiricists, sceptics and devout, understand the world. In a way, it is a necessary way of understanding anything. At the moment I am typing on my computer at my agreeable desk in London. Yet I believe that Vancouver exists at the same time. Do I have proof of this? Of course I can provide it: the testimony of others, a reliance on my own memories, and the evidence of innumerable websites and text books. Vancouver is, I am fairly sure, an existent thing.

But that belief rests on assumptions about the veracity of the testimony of others, including myself. Is it likely that I am the victim of an enormous Cartesian conspiracy designed to snare my poor feeble senses into the belief in a Canadian coastal Shangri-la? Of course I don't believe it. Can I prove it? Of course not. That's the point: we rely on varying degrees of doubt. If you're waiting for certainty before you commit to any belief, may I point out that you'll be waiting for some time. It certainly isn't a requirement in law, where at different times beyond reasonable doubt and the merely probable are both points at which verdicts can be delivered.

So it is with teaching, and human beings in particular. The simple belief that someone is capable, that some heights are possible, may not be confirmed by pointlessly specific and periodic dipsticks thrust into the class work. Sometimes the teacher needs to endure periods of faith, almost like a fast of certainty, in order to achieve the results of which some are capable. And often he will be disappointed. And often he will not. Which teacher would you rather have in charge of your children?

The patient man endures the abyss, and believes in the possibility of better things.

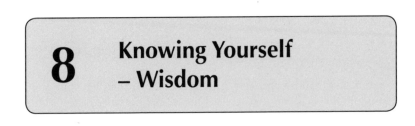

8 Knowing Yourself
– Wisdom

'SO, WHAT DID YOU DO BEFORE JOINING OFSTED?'

In Gideon the LORD appeared to Solomon in a dream by night: and God said, Ask what I shall give thee.

And Solomon said … Give therefore thy servant an understanding heart to judge thy people, that I may discern between good and bad: for who is able to judge this thy so great a people?

And the speech pleased the Lord … Behold, I have done according to thy words: lo, I have given thee a wise and an understanding heart; so that there was none like thee before thee, neither after thee shall any arise like unto thee.

– 1 Kings 3.5–12. King James Bible

Almost every wise saying has an opposite one, no less wise, to balance it.

– George Santayana

Wisdom is far more apparent in demonstration than by definition. I know that a man who has coated his tender member in egg white and bread crumbs doing naked squats above a pan of boiling oil is being unwise. I know that people who sleep in hyperbaric chambers are unwise. But what do they have in common?

Fortunately, wiser men than I have considered this, probably most famously Socrates (although we can never be sure; all of what we know about Socrates comes from his student Plato, as Socrates wrote nothing down). Socrates was described by the Oracle at Delphi as the wisest man alive. Perplexed (and probably, let's face it, incredibly smug), he tried in his usual method to establish what this meant. So he travelled around asking people what wisdom was, especially if they were people who traditionally were said to possess it.

A strange thing happened: he found that the people who were supposed to be wisest, upon Socratic interrogation, were proven to know … well, bugger all really; not what they claimed, and far less than they thought. Eventually (and somewhat pleasingly) Socrates came away from these conversations with the slightly arch idea that to be wise means to know that one is essentially lacking in knowledge: the famous, 'The beginning of wisdom is first to accept that one does not know anything.' This isn't an invitation for everyone to start competing to be the thickest person in the room, and therefore conversely the smartest. Rather, it is seen to be an admission that the essence of wisdom is to be wary of exceeding your epistemological limits. This definition of wisdom is called *Epistemic Humility.*

The problem with this as solution is that there are plenty of people who do not believe themselves to be wise – and rightly so, because they aren't. Admitting a lack of wisdom is a sign of humility for sure, but sometimes humility is justified, rather than being a pleasant way of making talented people bearable to be with.

What else could wisdom be? Some have claimed that what it really means is to be confident about the things that we genuinely do know, and not the things we'd like to claim we know. We can call this epistemic accuracy. But again there is a problem – lots of people think (and genuinely believe) that they know lots on a topic when they don't. Exhibit A: *Twitter.*

Aristotle develops this theory: wisdom is knowledge, knowing a good deal about a good deal. On the surface this is an attractive theory, as we commonly associate those we deem wise with those who know many things. But of course this fades when we consider the number of people who may possess a surfeit of knowledge, but we wouldn't trust them to be particularly wise. I mean, I'd want Gyles Brandeth on my Pub Quiz Team, but would you trust him to look after your kids for five minutes?[1]

To counter this, Aristotle makes a distinction between two types of wisdom: practical and theoretical. Theoretical is the one we could identify with knowledge: to know a lot. Practical wisdom is when we see it put into practice; that recognizes when a fact is useful; that knows when knowledge is useful, relevant and important. It is far closer to comprehension and understanding than it is to mere memorization. But before anyone jumps up and claims that Aristotle supports skills versus content, I would reiterate that skills are non-existent without content: to be wise about something is to know a great deal about it, and to be able to put that knowledge to sound effect. It is useless to have memorized the blueprint of a bomb if one doesn't know to get out of the way when it starts to tick.

Nozick recognizes this problem, as does Aristotle, when he develops his theory in the Nichomachean ethics. Wisdom (practical wisdom) is that which enables us to live well; the correct identification of what is important in order for us to realize our aims, and the intelligence to recognize what those aims should be. This is the heart of virtue ethics, and it is only right that as a definition it should be at the heart of the most important virtue.

Nozick clarifies this:

Wisdom is not just one type of knowledge, but diverse. What a wise person needs to know and understand constitutes a varied list: the most important goals and values of life – the ultimate goal, if there is one; what means will reach these goals without too great a cost; what kinds of dangers threaten the achieving of these goals; how to recognize and avoid or minimize these dangers; what different types of human beings are like in their actions and motives (as this presents dangers or opportunities); what is not possible or feasible to achieve (or avoid); how to tell what is appropriate when; knowing when certain goals are sufficiently achieved; what limitations are unavoidable and how to accept them; how to improve oneself and one's relationships with others or society; knowing what the true and unapparent value of various

---

[1] You would? Are you Gyles Brandeth?

things is; when to take a long-term view; knowing the variety and obduracy of facts, institutions and human nature; understanding what one's real motives are; how to cope and deal with the major tragedies and dilemmas of life, and with the major good things too.

(1989, p. 269)

To be wise is to understand one's role, and one's goal in one's community, and to realise what one must be and do in order to achieve those goals. A man who wishes to marry a girl should avoid dating her sister; an athlete, if he is wise, should train every day; a student, if she is wise, will hit the books and listen to teacher. This then appears to offer us a guide to what we mean by wisdom. It is inherently practical, because it is aimed at successful actions; it is based on character because it is an abstract and rational process of evaluating and identifying objects and processes that reach out towards aims and outcomes that require speculation, imagination and creative thinking.

I could conclude with this general estimation by adding that the final attribute of wisdom is that it is put into practice: that it can only really exist when it is actualized. A chain-smoker who considers himself to be wise because he continues to hide five boxes of reds a day in his lungs but knows 'all about the dangers' isn't really being wise at all, according to Aristotle; instead, he is merely deluding himself; or worse, he doesn't actually know the effects of smoking – sure, he might know intellectually (theoretical wisdom) but he doesn't really understand the true tragedy of an early painful death.

This is why any discussion of what wisdom is must be connected to a conversation about what the aims and roles are of the person under discussion. Wise advice isn't universally applicable – what is wise for one person to do may not be wise for another. If you're auditioning for a place in *Starlight Express*, then you would be wise to work the stage like John Barrowman; I would hardly recommend the same tactic for the man forced onto a window ledge by the Cosa Nostra. Wisdom is related to context, and also to one's role.

We've already discussed what the role of the teacher is: the question now is, what is wisdom within that role? With the benefit of the preceding discussion we are in a clearer place to discuss what this would mean and what it would look like.

Wisdom, in the context of teaching, means being able to identify the actions and routes necessary in order to be successful as a teacher. This is a broad definition, but necessarily so. A teacher needs to be wise in many contexts and ways, in order to realize his or her ambitions within the classroom and beyond (but I'll focus on within the school at least; what wisdom means for humans in general is entirely another story, and for that I recommend you to Mr Aristotle directly, and his commentators, and make up your own mind. I will stick to teaching).

Wisdom as the unifying, defining characteristic of the teacher

There is no more important attribute in a teacher than wisdom. This is because:

1. It supersedes all the other virtues; it allows the teacher to identify correctly when other virtues are required, and for how long.
2. Alone amongst the qualities of a teacher, it is dedicated and intrinsically aimed at the ultimate aims and goals of being a teacher. All other virtues – courage, fortitude and the rest – can be displayed in excess and deficiency; wisdom alone suffers no excess, only deficiency. And alone amongst the virtues it sees the teacher as a holistic entity, with overriding purposes and successes. Teacher wisdom is solely aimed at being a successful teacher.

We have already looked at courage etc. as necessary qualities to be a successful teacher. But what discerns the correct amount of courage, at what time, and in what context? Wisdom. Where do we find the internal timer that rings when patience has reached its natural and useful end, or pauses long enough to allow us to know when a pause hasn't been long enough? Wisdom.

Wisdom in the classroom

Wisdom is the attribute that allows us to understand the bigger picture of what is going on in the class. In my experience, broadly speaking, noisy classes learn less than ones that can be quiet on a regular basis; I find this axiom in the simple truth that being quiet allows one to listen and to think, and to write and to work without distraction. But this is not always the case: some activities require noise; some thrive because of it, like debates or hot-seating. Wisdom is the ability to remember that a noisy class might not be the worst thing in the world; to take a step back and ask oneself, what is the aim of the task I have set these students? And if the answer isn't impeded by the noise they produce, then wisdom asks, is the noise so bad after all?

In this context, wisdom is a way of seeing the forest and not focusing on the bark of the trees. I don't like kids talking when I'm talking, or when I've set quiet work for the class. But if I've just got a kid back into the class after a lengthy time out of school for delinquency, and he's working hard, and he suddenly and quietly asks the guy next to him for a pen, I'm not going to jump on him for breaking a class rule – that would be unwise; that would provoke a confrontation, and ruin the reintegration for no benefit whatsoever, in order to correct a rule infringement that nobody but me had noticed anyway. In other words, wisdom is a way of focusing on what you really want from a class, rather than simply losing oneself in the moment and thwarting your own ambitions.

Wisdom allows us to discern error, and admit it

Wisdom is also seen in the classroom when a teacher realizes that things aren't going well and a new tack needs to be taken. In any lesson, a good teacher should realize roughly what will happen and in what order – I believe it's called structure. And if you're being observed, either internally[2] or externally, then the teacher will develop a tendency to hang on to the lesson structure as planned with dear life and both hands. But every teacher will also have met the lesson where things didn't work: maybe their IT went tits-up;[3] maybe the kids didn't understand what you were trying to say; maybe there were so many of them out on a school trip that you couldn't run your debate. Whatever it was, there will always be times when the learning of the class simply isn't provided for by what you've prepared. Wisdom allows you to take the broader view, and invites you to can what you've prepared and maybe freestyle it a bit in order to get where you want them to go. Or perhaps you realize that where you want them to go is somewhere entirely different from where they were heading in the first place; maybe it's farther than you expected. Whatever, you need to be wise enough to know that fulfilling your stated aims might now be of subordinate importance to the new aim. Big picture. Small world.

---

[2] I don't mean by a gynaecologist or something.
[3] Say it isn't so.

The wisdom of the teacher/student relationships

This ability to discern utility from decoration and the effective from the merely whimsical is just as essential in the way you interact with students. There is, and always will be, a tension that exists between general rules for everyone to follow and exceptions to those rules depending on circumstances.

For example, every decent classroom will have general rules about conduct and behaviour, at least for reference when they are broken. But equally every teacher will have spotted times when exceptions could – or in fact should – be made. A police officer is perfectly within his rights to arrest a speeding motorist and give them the third degree. But should the officer do this to a man driving his heavily pregnant wife to hospital as the baby crowns? Of course not – he should get the blue light on and provide an escort, breaking every limit as he goes. No rule refuses all exception, because life isn't like that.

Similarly, the teacher needs to have the wisdom to realize when the greater ends of education are served by enforcing rules and when they are not. I might tactically ignore certain misbehaviours if this allows greater goals to be achieved. This isn't the tragic melancholy of compromise; this is life, or perhaps it is both. But more importantly it is a necessary part of life to realize that not all goals can be simultaneously achieved, and to think otherwise is childish. In a teacher, childish isn't a good look.

Of course, the natural fear is that when we put rules aside and admit exceptions, we dig a grave for ourselves, as others leap on the opportunity to point out that if exceptions can be made for one ... then why not another? Why not all? Soon the rule fades from existence and relativity is all. This too is an impossible route to take in human conduct: laws, for all their imperfections, govern the conduct of a community, providing a blueprint and a skeleton for social conduct to be possible. We do not set it aside lightly. But just as the whole institution of Law doesn't evaporate when the police officer sets compassion over compunction, so too can the wise teacher preserve boundaries and circumscription while occasionally stepping over the line. The trick is to know when, how often and for how long, just as it is in any circumstance that demands virtue, judgment and character.

How is this learned? In the same way that other virtues are:

1. By observation: we see others act, and we then evaluate how effective their actions were in achieving the end they desired.

Sometimes this is in itself an act of wisdom, as the 'results' of our actions are often subject to interpretation. If a teacher lets a pupil off lightly for failing to hand in homework, on the basis that there are problems at home, and in the hope that a kind word will instil the student with renewed vigour to complete the next task, how do we evaluate the effectiveness of this call? Of course, we could take the blunt answer and say, 'By judging the future behaviour of the pupil – how much homework was handed in, etc.' But this is a judgment call in itself – after all, how do we know the student would have acted if a more punitive response had been given after the homework failure? Maybe that would have inspired them even more. The answer is that we can never know the consequences of actions *not* taken, because alternative timelines aren't available for our inspection.[4] We have to make a judgment on the relationship between cause and effect, and consider that judgment over time and examples, making another judgment in turn about how they are related.

Practising this is a slow and arduous process that requires you to be patient, broad-minded and cautious in your conclusions. But then, nobody ever said the acquisition of wisdom was an easy process. Its value (and its rarity, surely) lies in the difficulty we find in mining it from the hard ground of experience.

2. By trying things yourself – in this case, the observation process will require even more tenacity and perspective. Ask yourself what you did, and what happened as a result. So you shouted at a noisy class – did it work? What else happened? Did they treat you with more disdain afterwards, or did it make them respect/fear you a bit more. Only you can tell. Try it again, and see what happens, with different students in slightly (or broadly) different circumstances. What happened this time? And try again. Teachers – in fact anyone who deals with humans for a living – needs to be a social scientist, while accepting that there will always be enormous limits and biases involved in the collation of information that is relevant to forming a conclusion.

3. By reading books like this.[5] Good luck with that, incidentally. This is why Aristotle emphasized the role of practical wisdom

---

[4] I have checked this exhaustively.
[5] Thank you for enabling me to build another wing on to my Maldivian mansion.

– theory and experience have to be absorbed and processed in equal measure, and while immersing yourself in educational literature is an excellent start (particularly if they are written by a well-meaning Glaswegian chancer), there is only so far you can learn to ride a bike by listening to a podcast. Eventually you have to straddle the saddle.[6] But books can offer you food for thought – possible points to reflect upon, and suggestions about where you went wrong, or were right. That's my ontological justification, anyway. Actually I'm just in it for the fame and glory.[7]

So watch, practise, reflect, repeat. That's the way we acquire wisdom in this, as in any field. You can probably guess my feelings on the opinions of others who have never taught, or stood inside a classroom in a meaningful way, when they feel fit to pronounce on the way I should teach; the list includes (unfortunately) many educationalists, government ministers, LEA advisors, newspaper journalists, and just about everyone who appears to have significant amounts of input into the way that schools are created, run, assessed and organized. To paraphrase Chris Hitchens, hearing a non-teacher tell me how to teach kids is like a virgin telling me how to f*ck.

The next person who comes up to me and tells me what children *really* need in a classroom gets a free set of five fingers curled up into an amusing ball, delivered with speed. I don't tell astrophysicists how to track quasars, and I'm not bothered by people with degrees in journalism or business telling me how to run a classroom. Quote me.

---

6 As the janitor said to the SENCO.
7 You have to be joking. Of course.

EXCLUSION MEETING

'IN MY DEFENCE I'D LIKE TO SUBMIT THAT MY PREFERRED LEARNING STYLE INVOLVES BEING SURLY AND SELFISH.'

I must be cruel only to be kind

– William Shakespeare

Compassion has many names and leads to many places; but at its root, the specific atomic number to which I refer is the feeling of empathy and sympathy one has for another; the ability to imagine the pain and delight of another, and to consider that meaningful and important; it is also the key ingredient in altruism, the desire to see good come to another apart from yourself.

Note that there are at least two components to this: one intellectual, one emotional. The second is probably the easier to grasp – the feeling one experiences when we are moved by the suffering or otherwise of others and the desire to see that suffering ended or wellbeing extended. This is a non-rational state; it varies according to our peculiar sensibilities at the time, and how we feel towards another in a specific context. It changes as our feelings change and is unreliable, though undoubtedly powerful. In 1985 I, along with millions of others around the world watched Live Aid, Bob Geldof's antidote to sadness and poverty. At one point a fund-raising video was played by Michael Burke, reporting from Ethiopia's famine; over his silent end-footage, somebody played the undoubtedly mawkish and self-pitying hymn 'Drive' by The Cars. Pompous and trite it may have been, but there weren't many dry eyes in the living-rooms of the nation there, or in Wembley Stadium, afterwards. And of course, phone donations (or 'fockin' phone' donations as Sir Bob put it) soared in the minutes afterwards. Compassion, the emotion that moves us to allay the sorrow of others.

This emotional state is unreliable; five minutes before the appeal, how strongly did I feel towards the plight of the Ethiopians? And five months after? But all emotions suffer from this characteristic.

The second aspect of compassion is held in the head. This is a cooler beast, but no less important – it is the knowledge that one wills the good for another, even if you aren't 'feeling it' at the time. Joseph Fletcher called this version *agape* in his philosophy of Situation Ethics: the unconditional knowledge of love, the attitude of love towards someone else. It can easily be expressed in the old Gospel adage of 'Love your neighbour as yourself', and it could have easily added the appendix, 'Even when you don't feel like it'.[1]

We're all familiar with this kind of love. If you have a screaming child at three in the morning taking you away from dream time,

---

[1] They really missed a trick there. I'm just saying.

or sexy time, or whatever time that isn't feeding baby time, you'll understand. Do you still love your child? Yes. Are you feeling that love in a way that could be described as tender and soft? Probably not. It's an attitude you hold, a general preference, a relationship towards someone else. It isn't just an emotional state. It can't be, unless you want your love to be something that flickers and flares according to the time of day, the right night, the candlelight or Barry White. Try it: the next time your partner asks you, 'Do you love me?' why not answer, 'Well, let me see; I'll just check with my internal emotional state.' See how long your relationship lasts.

But important though the attitudinal aspect of this is, it is unsustainable without the succour of the emotional. It is probably impossible to maintain an attitude of love and compassion towards someone if you *never* feel the emotional aspect of that love at any point; well, maybe some people can, but the last time somebody could they nailed him to a tree and stole his coat. Mere mortals need a combination of the two.

The importance of compassion in education

The idea that compassion is an important virtue to have in teaching is simultaneously obvious and controversial. It is, after all, a profession where the wellbeing of others is part of the intrinsic aim of the role. You are there to better the education of the children in your charge, and that is automatically directed towards others. What could be more compassionate than that? Well, for a start teachers haven't always been associated with the engines of delight and charm that we now know them to be; in fact it would be fair to say that until the second half of the twentieth-century, many people's experiences of formal education would have been characterized equally with punishment and discomfort as with cuddles. Or to put it another way, there are many, many times when you will walk into (or out of) a classroom, and the predominant emotion you feel will not be a beautiful acknowledgement of the brotherhood of man.

A more interesting dilemma many face is that some would say that in order to be a teacher, an adult, an authority and a professional, it is best if one doesn't suffer too much compassion, and that one should treat students with a dispassionate regard for nothing other than their academic wellbeing. Others say that being a teacher requires constant emotional compassion, with empathy and understanding as a necessary if not a sufficient condition of the profession.

These are false dichotomies; they all contain germs of the truth. It is impossible to separate any enterprise that involves other people from the emotional and intellectual aspects of compassion. It will exist in varying levels, but it will exist. The key question for teachers is this: how much do you need to have, how much is appropriate, and why is it important? Note that I don't just say useful, but important. So why?

Compassion was described by David Hume as a 'natural well of sympathy towards the suffering of others'. He thought that morality was essentially an invention of society, and that this natural human tendency was the best; the only – way to justify being kind to one another – it was appropriate to our species. It was a matter of fact rather than a God-given moral command. Whatever it is – the product of efficiency, a social contract, a divine edict – compassion is the great catalyst of our human nature. In its absence we are separated from each other; viciousness is only one of it's deficiencies.

Its proper deficiency isn't spite or cruelty, but an absence of care or unconcern. Just as I am unmoved by the fate of rivers on Mars or anything else that has no impact or meaning for me, the lack of compassion prevents us from seeing others in the same category as ourselves. Kant said that self-love was a proper and present part of the human condition, and this is probably true. It is also invariably true that we don't hold others in as high a regard as we do ourselves, no matter how altruistic we try to be. I mean, I *care* what you have for lunch, and I hope you enjoy it, but really, I'm more worried about what I'm going to have.[2] When I lay me down to sleep at the end of the night, I plump my own pillows, not yours (I hope; apologies if I'm wrong).

Mr Christ was probably on to something when he said, 'Greater love hath no man than this, that a man lay down his life for his friends.' Because there isn't – the act of self-sacrifice, whether it be the literal act of throwing oneself onto a grenade or the metaphorical act of crushing your ambitions and opportunities to salvage the hopes of another (an act well-known to parents and carers everywhere) is both an act of self-annihilation and an awesome display of nerve and love. To subjugate oneself deliberately and intelligently for the good of another displays self-restraint that puts the cardio-trickery of the Swami or the Gurus to shame.

Compassion is a critical element of teachers. Their entire career is focused on the wellbeing of others. This is an intrinsic, conceptual

---

[2] Probably a Pot Noodle.

foundation. The job isn't to stand in a room and talk about verb forms and trigonometry – the role is to teach others. It is unavoidable. Compassion follows this path, directed out, away from oneself and towards the lives of others. If the actions of the teacher are not directed towards this goal, then it is not teaching; it is something else, and I don't have a name for it. There are many reasons why one would wish to be a teacher, and some of them are bad reasons. I know teachers who appear to be in classrooms because it's raining outside, and the children are seemingly impediments to them having a quiet nap at their desk. There are teachers who appear not to give a damn if their children learn or not, so long as the minutes tick by and wages are paid in to bank accounts. Fortunately such creatures are rare. Such teachers rarely enjoy success, and they certainly don't enjoy their professional careers, which are seen as obstacles to their eventual happiness doing ... what? I have no idea. And neither do they.

The vice of deficiency, and the temptations to succumb

Compassion is also important for the teacher because it is a virtue that directs us to put others before us, that motivates and supports us when the temptation to act selfishly is strong. And to be sure the temptations are there:

1. Teaching can be intoxicating for some – being in front of others, being the sole focus of attention, enjoying the exaggerated sense of importance that authority and position can bring .... these are all dangerous temptations to the teacher. Often such people lack acknowledgement and regard in their own lives, and rarely achieve such levels of popularity in any other context. It is like being a very, very tiny rock star. This drug can lead teachers to start to need the fix of adulation or at least attention. But the children are not there to adore the teacher; the teacher is there for them. To use children as a means to salve one's self-regard is a foul thing, although many fall into it accidentally.

2. If you've had a bad day, you know how easy it is to drag it like a reeking pelt into the classroom, showing it off to everyone. If you're really feeling hard done by, you can take it out on the children – detentions escalate, as your righteous mood lashes out at normally angelic children. This is an abuse of your role: you are there for them, not the other way around.

3. If you're chasing better grade point averages or you have a target of A-C passes that you're aiming for, you can be tempted to focus on certain groups of children only – for example, borderline D/C candidates, because after all they're the ones with which you can achieve most success. The brainy kids will pass anyway; the dumb kids are a lost cause. The pass mark is all. This is foul, even Stygian. This subordinates the needs of the children to the needs of your CV. *You*, remember, are there for *them*.

The excess of compassion: smother love

Can you ever be too compassionate? Some religions and eastern 'philosophies'[3] would hold that God is love; some cultural traditions would tell us that love is all you need; a many-splendoured thing; the greatest gift, etc. I would counsel caution with all such prospectuses. The older I get the more I come to a very simple and utterly unprovable maxim – that love is the most important guiding force in the human universe. That it provides the aim and the reason for being alive. I cannot intellectualize or reason this any more clearly than that; I certainly cannot offer you a demonstration, mathematical, logical or empirical. I simply believe this to be true because in the rare moments when I see clearly, I see this truth clearly also. I admit the failings of this of an argument, but then it isn't one. It is a truth known to myself, and I find it self-evident as much as I find the consciousness of my own existence true.

But (and the preceding is irrelevant to my reasoning, which means that what follows is communicable and concrete) there are dangers in compassion too: perhaps not directly by its excess, but by it dominating over other virtues; by failing to recognize that compassionate acts that take no account of other elements of human existence can fail to satisfy the aim of compassion. In other words, compassion is not our only compass. There are other Pole Stars.

Doing something purely for the benefit of others; this is perhaps the easiest rock to notice as we navigate through compassion. There are innumerable things I could do for the perceived benefit of others that might be harmful or to the detriment of others besides myself (self-sacrifice is one thing; to sacrifice another, especially an unwilling

---

[3] Those are 'irony commas' incidentally. Eastern philosophy resembles philosophy in the same way that a Creme Egg has anything to do with chickens.

participant, is entirely another). I could bring a junkie a bag of rock crystal with which to smoke the day away. As an activity directed towards another's desires, it has no peer; as an act of genuine altruism, it leaves a lot to be desired. Of course, this illustrates that there are things we desire and things that are to our benefit, and it is this distinction that is most important in teaching.

Learning can be enormous fun; it can also be enormously dry. There it is, and that's an end to it. Those who say that all learning and all lessons must engage or entertain are, to be honest, a bit simple. I regard them as well-meaning but essentially quite stupid. The job of the teacher is to direct the children through education; to teach them the best that we have learned so far, to enable them to exceed us, to exceed even themselves. But what it *isn't* always is enjoyable. And it is perfectly normal (in fact I would be worried if it wasn't) for a child at times to resist the delights of the classroom. In other words, sometimes some children won't enjoy doing as they're told. I do hope this isn't a shock.

But as teachers, our job, our duty is to do exactly this: to consider the long-term interests of the child even if they themselves do not perceive the benefit. I know that if I have some pretty tight, fair rules in my class, if we can all co-operate with me as an authoritative centre, then we can all learn in a more engaging and safe way; we can all get on with it, with a minimum of fuss and shouting, detentions and sanctions. Many small children do not realize this; or they choose not to; or they reckon that they're the most important things in the room. They are perfectly welcome to have these illusions. My role exists whatever they think; to guide, to protect, to teach, and that's what I'll bloody well do, whether they want it or not. Education isn't optional (unless you count the option of parents to home educate, and quite right too); the curriculum isn't open for debate (except at the most senior levels in the QCA, or at the departmental level as curricula are discussed and adopted). These are not things for the students or the parents to decide. A lot of it is out of our hands, and in the hands of ministers and Demos.

The compassionate response to this situation is to teach what we know as well as we can, using the best rules that we can. It means at times enforcing boundaries, and patrolling those boundaries frequently. It means punitive, distributive and retributive justice. It means doing all these things even if the students whine and wheeze and hiss and howl … because we care about them. It is the administration of what is often called tough love, because love is not always soft – sometimes it is hard. The judge sentencing the criminal does not (or perhaps should not) feel pleasure in the act; it is done because it is necessary. A country raising its arm to defend itself from unprovoked attack shouldn't feel a joy in doing so – it should be treated as a necessary act of self-love. A surgeon doesn't flinch when he cuts into a patient (surely an obvious exception to Hippocrates' maxim, 'First, do no harm') because he knows that the cut is a precursor to the cure.

Boundaries and compassion

There is no contradiction between compassion and boundaries. Rather, they are necessary principles of each other. Compassion without restriction can lead to disastrous permissiveness – the desire to seek someone's good, if not tempered by reference to other, equally important principles such as long-term wellbeing and safety can result in indulged, spoiled children who know no sense of restriction. If you've ever seen a child with dark mossy holes where their teeth should be then you know how the story will end if you allow children to follow their dietary desires. And we've all seen the impact that needless, incessant indulgences can have on a single child, and you don't have to be familiar with the fate of Verucca Salt[4] to know where all that ends up. Self-restraint is a necessary component of any success or scheme that relies on short-, mid-, and long-term goals and few worthwhile things spring successfully into life ex nihilo, unless you're a patron of national lotteries or magic lamps. Even then.

Boundaries are necessary for compassion, and compassion is essential in deciding boundaries. They are constructed in order to act as ladders and scaffolding for children to climb higher than they could ever have dared to dream. Absolute licentiousness isn't associated with freedom but with tyranny; enslavement to whims, to selfish wants, to desires and to indolence. And it is only by suffering the chafe of restriction that we can taste sweet freedom. All things are discerned by their opposites – light is only understood when darkness is possible; good is known through the presence of evil; delight is only discovered through the knowledge of disaster, and only a hungry man truly understands appetite. I realize that this is beginning to sound a bit 'freedom through slavery' but I don't follow this maxim through to that unnecessary conclusion, because the opposites aren't identical – but they are related.

---

[4] Deserving victim of ignoring Health and Safety directives at Mr Wonka's legendary confectionery plant.

Compassion in the classroom

One of the reasons that every teacher should consider this virtue carefully is because I have seen an extraordinary number of teachers – particularly new teachers – who appear to believe that love, and love alone, will transform their classrooms. I mean, that's a fine sentiment, but then so is believing in yourself and never giving up on your dreams, and I don't want to make that the guiding maxim of my life either. Love and compassion are an energy that can blast empires into atoms, but its transformative power is found in its ability to change YOU, not other people. One stalwart NQT I knew was bloody delighted to be entering the profession. She knew that the school was tough, but she didn't care. 'When I was at school,' she said, 'The teachers just didn't care about us at all; well, I do – I care about these kids, and I'm going to show them that I want to make a difference to them.'

Three weeks later and she was a certified wreck. The kids had taken her boundless love, her intricately planned lessons and her endless, bottomless enthusiasm for her subject and for them, and told her to shove them up her arse. She wore sandals, you see, and they didn't take to her. Besides, she was new, and they liked her a deal less than her predecessor. That's awful, isn't it? Well, there you go; that's how it happens sometimes. All the love in the world didn't make a bit of difference. And what was worse, her certainty that compassion alone would renovate their ambitions towards academia made it unbearable. Couldn't they see, she would wail, that she cared about them? They didn't care.

Too much loving? The excess of compassion

And it reminds me of another danger of compassion in excess, or held as a transformative universal rather than a vital ingredient in a bigger picture: the indisputable fact that we can only be hurt by the ones we love. And it's true, isn't it? If a stranger, or better, if someone you hold in little regard, calls you a blackheart, or a batty, or indeed, even a *blud-clart*, do you care? Well, you might, but only in a sort of 'isn't that strange?' way. But if that same comment came from a friend then you would be reeling from the dagger in your heart.

Faithful are the wounds of a friend – but the kisses of the enemy are deadly

The teacher must care for – love his children; must care for their well-being; especially their academic wellbeing must often put their needs before his or her own, recognizing that there will be tensions between these two states. But, as much as humanly possible, there must be a limit to that love; there has to be a professional distance that creates a barrier, however thin, between the teacher and the pupil. There has to be. Otherwise the emotional shock will devastate you.

Compare this to the role of a nurse. Every day, most nurses deal with patients that just don't get better; that waste away, or expire in distressing and messy ways. Often these are patients that the nurse has spoken to for days, weeks and sometimes months. They may be on good terms and share stories and jokes. And then the nurse has to watch that person die. And minutes later, when most of us would be grieving, or recovering, or sharing our grief with family and friends, they have to attend to matters that would horrify us; cleaning the body, changing the bed, finally moving on to another patient and other potential heartaches. New nurses often crumble under the strain; experienced nurses have learned to deal with it. Simple evolution demands that they have to: cope or leave. So they build up a barrier between themselves and their patients, not based on cruelty, but on the willed ability to keep patients at just the right distance to help them best. This is the kind of compassion that teachers need to learn.

Care about them; but try to do so in a general *agape* way, to hold them in regard because they are worthy of love, and your time and effort. But just as you can't weep all summer for the students who leave every year, you can't bury yourself in a bottle when a student underperforms, truants or insults you. Why? Because they do not love you, usually; because they do not take your criticisms home and cry themselves to sleep over them; because to them you are an adult and a teacher, but not their mums and dads, and certainly not the most important adult in their lives. You can be, for some, but this is not the norm; you are part of their lives – you are not the centre of their universe. This is why some of them can so easily curse and chasten you – because you mean a lot less to them than they do to themselves. You need to maintain a distance from them while still loving them. This is a balancing act, and not easy to pull off, but this is the trick of teaching: to balance love and dispassion; to maintain professionalism in a field that is innately personal. It is a skill learned over time, partly intellectually, partly intuitively.

This barrier will save you an enormous amount of heartache when children don't immediately respond to your compassion in a way that you would expect from a reasonable adult – in other words, YOU. But it will also allow you to apply that compassion in a more measured, considered way. It almost seems contradictory to talk about reasonable emotions and measured reactions, but there is an interplay between these two things. Compassion, if applied emotionally and without restraint to your pupils, will leave you bruised and burnt; worse, it can make you bitter, hurt that the tender sentiment of your good will has been so easily and maliciously cast aside. This bitterness can easily simmer into resentment – they, after all, have shown that they don't deserve you, and that is the death of compassion.

But compassion, as we have seen, has a cooler component than the hot lava that flows through the chambers of our heart: it also has a faculty of being understood, directed and justified. If you maintain this barrier between you and your charges, you can observe as children say churlish things to you, or ignore you, or defy you, and still understand that your principal duty to them is compassion, without having that sense of compassion destroyed by insult, injury or pique. It's the same as when you need to rebuke a student: you can portray anger without feeling anger. Similarly there will be times when you administer and deliver compassion and love to your students, but frankly you won't be feeling much by way of love. This is professional compassion. In some ways it is a stunt, and in others it is profound and genuine. It is a paradox of something as inherently paradoxical as the sense of empathizing with another that is not yourself. It is intrinsically non-rational, but also a function of rationality; it is brave, it is selfless, it is love.

10 The Vices of the Profession

I thought I would also focus on some of the vices of character that teachers can also demonstrate. Some of them I've discussed already – cruelty, cowardice, complacency – but I thought it would be valuable for us to consider the kind of bad habits that we, as teachers, can fall into. Some of these happen by accident, some of them by experience and lack of judgment, so I'll look at some of them together here.

Laziness

The curse of kings and vagabonds; the great leveller. *I cannot be arsed* must be one of the most commonly felt, if not expressed, sentiments that informs and motivates (or rather doesn't) the human condition, and I don't care what Paolo Coelho says. 'Nature,' Jeremy Bentham, the great Utilitarian social philosopher once wrote, 'has placed mankind under two sovereign masters: pain and pleasure.' On a crude, but real level (and let's face it, reality sometimes is crude) we seek one and recoil from the other. Yet experience and all kinds of psychology teach us that we are far more inclined to avoid discomfort than we are actively to seek out pleasure. The natural state of mankind, I have discovered after extensive testing on my sofa, is to be at rest, punctuated by short trips to the fridge and the bathroom. If science could somehow engineer an IV drip that could accommodate both, I imagine humanity would simply stop, so long as television was available to accommodate the twelve or so hours of consciousness in between naps. Did you hear that knocking? That's the *Planet of the Apes*, trying to get in, waiting its turn. I'm telling you.

All but the very neurotic are prey to this vice: the deficit of industry. And yet it is something that modern Western European democracies seem perfectly designed to accommodate. Previously, in civilization, downtime was a luxury afforded to the very few at the top of the pyramid, sometimes literally, while the lumpen proles mashed their fingers into strawberry jam building enormous geometric palaces and tombs for their more cunning masters, who justified their dominance on a series of claims based around divine right, genetic superiority and brute force.

I imagine that for the vast majority of the human race, for the vast majority of the history of our species, leisure time was simply the thing you did when you stopped working for a few hours and shut your eyes for a handful of hours in between shoveling shit. Don't think I'm joking. Historical period dramas portray the past as a wonderful place to be, which it probably was if you were the Duke of Buckingham or Genghis Khan. For everyone else, it was an unending stream of effluence raining on your head until the day it stopped, at which point you were churned into the vegetable patch for fertiliser. If I found a time machine I would fill it with kerosene and chuck in a match Sorry, Doctor.

Laziness is a vice peculiarly fit for the modern day in economies where, for the first time, we can produce more than we need, and the excess can exceed even the atavistic desires of the privileged class, trickling down into the lives of the unwashed, stunned masses who have suddenly found themselves through labour-saving devices, agriculture, animal husbandry and the division of labour, in a position where they can do more than provide grist for the factory mill and make duplicates of themselves, gifted to posterity. This is by no means a rant against the welfare state, or against societies that believe that the wealth of the nation should be shared for the benefit of all citizens, but it is an indication that laziness isn't a vice that one would presumably detect in the Serengeti desert, where the lazy already serve a purpose – lion bait.

Teachers succumb to this vice in equal measure to their other social counterparts; this might sound counter-intuitive, because as we all know teachers work frightfully, frightfully hard, and of course many/most of them do; this isn't the kind of job where there are a lot of opportunities to stand still and twiddle ones thumbs; a bell and five hundred children will testify to that. But laziness strikes in many, many other ways.

The first problem is when the teacher has developed their first series of lessons, and delivered it a few times. A good teacher will look at their schemes of work every year and think, 'Is that the best I can do? Does this need to be sharpened up a bit?' But often, after the exhausting first few years, many teachers simply pull up the handbrake and go for a fag break that lasts for the rest of their career.

I still see teachers using resources they wrote in their training year, and not in a good way, but in a 'that'll do' way. The idea that your lessons are somehow good enough after an induction period makes a mockery of the idea that teaching is a profession, and that we are constantly polishing our craft, which we should be if we want to be considered as a profession, rather than a collection of postmen for the latest fashionable ideology to emerge from the DfE.

The second kind of laziness is related to the first; it's the laziness of settling with how the students are doing. Again, most teachers really put gas in their tanks for the first few years, working out what works and what doesn't in the classroom – do I use a seating plan or not (answer: yes, incidentally); do I do paired work? Do I set detentions, etc? All of these questions get answered to varying degrees of efficiency as the training years progress. But for many teachers, that's enough; I once worked – incredibly – with a man who had taught for twenty years at the same boys' school, but even after all this time he still struggled with behaviour, still couldn't remember all their names, and still got grades that resembled a protein sequence, repeated endlessly: DEEF. Stubborn as a mule, he used to send them out of his lessons ten minutes early because he was 'fed up with them', which I imagine after twenty years of having the same day over and over, you would be. I was agog at the casualness with which he regarded his craft (of course he called it that, but it never appeared to be that for him in any way); he simply thought that the kids were vile, and if they didn't obey him that was their problem and why should he do anything about it? Never set detentions, never set homework he had to mark, never did anything other than the absolute minimum to survive. And I do mean *survive*.

That kind of laziness is extreme, but unfortunately shades of it shadow us all at times; you promise to return some homework, but don't because some fabulous reality show is on telly that night; you turn up late for a lesson because you want to finish off a game of Angry Birds, or a conversation, or a paragraph in your great new book. You stick on a DVD because you couldn't be bothered to plan a decent lesson. And so on, and so on.

I'm not advocating that we as teachers should be active as beetles on a pin or a hamster in a wheel – God, we're only human, even the ones who come through *Teach First* – but I think this is one of the chief vices that experienced teachers fall into, settling for the way things are; doing the same thing every year, surely creating a cage of boredom that suffocates. This is a job where you have to work hard to make it work. And every few years ask yourself, have I settled? Have

I gone down a gear? And for many of us the answer if we're honest is *yes*.

Cynicism

What a f*cking sh*t job this is. Kids are, let's be honest, an enormous pain in the ass, of Leviathan proportions. You can't borrow money from them. They are needy to the point of ridiculousness, collectively like an enormous nappy that constantly needs to be hand washed, while a car alarm goes off in the background, only instead of an alarm noise it's Drum and Bass[1] played through a megaphone. That's what kids are like. And the paperwork is a *joke*; you spend more time filling in reports on kids than you do planning lessons. And even when you do, you're not allowed to say anything true, just things like,'Sammy has been letting himself down lately', when Sammy has been a perpetual moron for the last six months, and letting himself down implies that there was an up in the first place from which he could descend. Parents are a nightmare, and you can see where the kids get it from. There's no point calling home because they'll just take the side of the maggots they produced a decade or so ago, grooming them so that they can be your personal tormentors.

Of course, senior staff are no help. They just sit in their remote offices and keep themselves comfy. Whenever I ask them to discipline a kid, they practically pat the kids on the head and give them a biscuit,. Then the kid's back with me next lesson, as if nothing has happened. Frankly, I just try to get through from one day to the next and wait until the term breaks start, because there's no fun in teaching, not anymore. It was different in the old days, of course. Kids used to respect teachers then. I don't set detentions or anything anymore, because frankly I'm sick of the reaction it causes, and they never turn up anyway. Plus, why should I have to waste my time to babysit them after school? That just puts me in detention too.

Teaching is a joke now. It's not teaching. It's child-minding. Society is going to the dogs, and now we're expected to be the ones who sort it all out? Don't make me laugh. The money's not that good, the pensions are being stripped away, and even the holidays aren't enough, because if we didn't have them then we'd go nuts. By the time they end, you've just about got yourself rested, and then the whole shit storm starts again. I don't know why I bother.

---

[1] Sorry: 'Drum 'n' bass'

And neither do I. Don't be this person; even if some of the complaints are legitimate, the response is not. Anyone that finds themselves in this mental frame of mind consistently, and genuinely believes it to be the case – if you read the preceding paragraphs and thought, yes, that's exactly what I think – get the hell out of the profession, because you're no good to the kids. Seriously, you're a danger. Better still if you try to improve things for yourself – try another school, or another style of teaching, or another phase or stage. But do not remain in a profession where your attitude and effort matters to the wellbeing of children. They deserve much, much better than this. It's an easy job in which to become cynical; any job that involves dealing with the public is a heartache at times, because for all the good will and professionalism in the world, some people just won't appreciate your efforts, especially when you're dealing with masses of strangers who frankly don't value you as much as they probably should. Don't take that out on everyone else. It's not the fault of the next year's cohort that the last one was mean to you. Just because a few parents are feral doesn't mean they all are. And just because others around (and I include some SLT of course) are rubbish doesn't mean that you give up.

I don't think that you should attempt to match a Disney Store employee for relentless optimism, but staying positive is essential in this career; you need to have a little faith in people; you need to be able to hope for the best from some students, because I guarantee that for many of these students, you will be the person who believes in them the most. Without you, there's no one, and they will be doomed to the inevitabilities of their statistical destiny. You are a link in the chain of their lives, and sometimes you're a stepping stone and sometimes a door mat (or you'll feel like it).

There are many things wrong in this profession, and until humans are perfected in some form of Omega evolutionary state, it seems impossible to conceive how it will ever be anything other than imperfect. But this is the argument of the defeated; things are awful, they always will be, so why bother trying to change anything? Why indeed? Why clean your teeth, or fill your belly? Why fall in love? Why help anyone? Why do anything at all, in fact, given the transience of even the longest-lived commodities; even diamonds will one day decay, and human lives are far, far more transient than the softest of stones. This is the argument of the suicide.

For the rest of us, who choose to remain conscious and alive, this is no argument. We do what we can; we might not be able to save the world from itself, but we can save the square metre directly in front of us, and someone else can save the square next to me, and perhaps we can benefit from it together. Perhaps not. We do our best for the children, and some will rise to the experience; some will exceed our expectations and us. And some will not; some will confound our efforts, and some will despise them, and that's OK too. That's life.

A siege mentality

There is no us and them in teaching, but you could be forgiven for thinking that teachers exist in a state of permanent siege; it is a profession, to be sure, where you can be perfectly alone in a crowd, as the majority of us operate in situations where we are the only adult in the room, and usually the only teacher. Once training is over, you will only see another grown-up in the room when it's some hard-on with a clipboard and an observation sheet. I often tell trainee teachers to really make the most of the supportive environment of the training year, when other teachers aren't just available, but required to be in the room with you at various points; it's a great way to reflect on what you're doing as a teacher, and it's a chance that evaporates once you achieve qualified teacher status – more's the pity – as it's an essential component in keeping your teaching fresh.

But it is easy – so, so easy – to start imagining that you are the only one who exists in school; that you are isolated and alone, the sole traveller of a solitary path, walking down the lost highway, etc. etc. It's an appealing, if slightly tired, anti-heroic trope. But it isn't/shouldn't be true. You are part of a teaching body, which is part of a greater staff body that, in mainstream education at least, is part of an enormous network of staff and resources. It's like you're part of the army. We are not Navy SEALS; we are soldiers in a unit. It just feels like we're alone. And to be fair, sometimes we are; but a teacher's strength lies in his ability to do what the children cannot: collaborate, and wait.

We play a long game, where insults and transgressions don't have to be resolved on the spot, but with time and patience; we also work with others to make this happen. We have no magical powers, and we certainly can't control their behaviour. What we do have is a collegiate power, which only exists when we rely on each other and support each other in turn. Never, never, never burden yourself by imagining that you are alone, and that the children are some hydra-headed opponent with forty arms and no brain.[2] Most children are amenable, and perfectly

---

[2] My little joke.

capable of responding well to being taught well; the minority who are not aren't exactly master criminals; their strength lies in their unusual confidence and extraordinary sense of entitlement, launching them into acts of anti-authoritarianism that some would find breathtaking.

These are the three steps to becoming powerful in school:

1. tell someone else what is going on
2. ask for help when you need it
3. follow up, and ask what is being done.

The vast majority of support staff and colleagues will, if handled properly, bend over backwards to help you. But you need to allow yourself to be part of that greater body. There are, of course, many staffs that are not as helpful as they should be; if this is the case, then you have to prod and poke them until they are, and if they still are not, you can either resolve to endure the lack of support, or take your services to a school where they value teachers. I recommend the latter.

Pettiness

I will define this as the sin whereby a teacher uses his or her role to score points, or to feed some dreadful demon within that can only be sated by the humiliation and vindication of children's opinions. I speak, of course, of the teacher who gets into arguments with children, or seeks to belittle them for some reason.

Of course, there are always reasons why we start to argue with children, few of them good; I am sure that most of us have been drawn into a needless tête-à-tête with a stroppy student at some point; it's practically irresistible (and inevitable) when your blood is up and someone is really, really trying to get in your face. But this isn't the kind of situation I'm describing. There are times when children say to me, 'Miss X hates me – she always picks on me!' and I usually soothe their troubled brows by contradicting their proposition, assuring them that they are not hated, and reminding them that they usually get in trouble for a multitude of sins (funny how it's usually the kids who spend all day mucking about on phones and bunking lessons who usually also claim they are being picked on. I'm not drawing any conclusions from that,[3] but you can draw your own and we'll just say no more).

---

[3] Heaven forbid.

But then there are some teachers (and I really am talking about a subtle few, but it's a problem nonetheless) who have been in the role so long that they start to see their relationships with the kids as meaningful to them in a personal sense – and usually a negative one. Of course, it's perfectly healthy (see Compassion) to develop professional feelings of compassion, concern and regard for the students, but they are not your pals. Similarly, it is entirely wrong to view them as enemies in any way. My God, there are at least a dozen students that I learned to detest as a teacher; it's impossible to avoid it, because you are human, despite what the manual tells you, and some personality types will simply rub you the wrong way. And some of them you may even loathe; my personal allergy is to children who want to become pop stars/rap stars/actors, but who display no discernible talent whatsoever other than the ability to replicate the loathsome egos of their role models. It really is a personal problem for me, and I admit it in the manner of an alcoholic at an intervention. But there you go, they're your students, so what can you do? Answer: treat them as you would any other student, or at least with a sense of neutral detachment. Avoid conversations with these people, and never, never, never get into arguments with them. For God's sake, what do you hope to achieve? What is the point of winning such an argument, even if you could. Do you expect the other kids to nod their heads approvingly and say something like, *Man, he be fly*? What are you the Fresh Prince of Bel Air?[4]

To adopt a famous aphorism, it's like winning the prize for best vegetable in show – you're still a vegetable. To attempt to argue, score points, humiliate or belittle one of your students shows a profound misinterpretation of the role you're supposed to inhabit. Of course, there will be people reading this thinking, 'How absurd! Only a fool would do this.' But it's far easier to discern poor practice in theory than it is to extract it from our practice. Any time you feel like coming back to a student with a sharp barb, or making someone look foolish at their expense, consider 'How would I feel if I were spoken to like this by a colleague?' Of course YOU don't do it. Nobody does. And yet they do.

---

[4] A role which I believe is already taken. Word.

Section Three: The Workout

Pumping iron

Aren't the virtues just a matter of opinion? I can only hold my hands up and agree; Aristotle found the same problem. Even he acknowledged that what was considered to be virtuous in one place/city state might not be seen as such somewhere else. The ancient Spartans, as all fans of crypto-history (as depicted by teen-friendly stylized Hollywood films) will confirm, believed that pride was enormously important as a virtue, the ability to be able to boast of one's magnificence. The Christian Church replaced it with humility as the operative virtue, thank God, or we'd still be listening to sandal-wearing generals boast about how many Carpathians they'd butchered on Sky News every night. Being humble was seen as an appropriate virtue for Christian, medieval society. Perhaps pride has returned to contemporary mores as a public asset; witness the braggadocio of contemporary celebrity culture.[1]

Does this suggest that there are different virtues for different cultures? What does this say about the integrity of those virtues? Can *anything* be a virtue and anything a vice, and are we doomed to moral relativism, where anything and nothing is right or wrong?

Not quite.

We are still talking about the role of a teacher here; and we are still talking about the education of human beings, who to some extent are the same organisms as they have been for the last few hundred thousand years or so. There is nothing to suggest that the way people learn these days is substantially biologically or psychologically different from the way that Moses would have learned 3,500 years ago. I know that this drives IT advocates loopy, or people who believe that children can only learn if we download information

---

[1] Does that make me sound like Judge Pickles? 'What is a muppet, exactly?' etc.

directly into their cerebral cortex via the language of ultra-dub or something, but it's true. Learning is still much the same shape it always has been. Anyone suggesting that vast new paradigms now exist which challenge the basic structure of education are talking out of their colons. You may *wish* it to be true – it may make them substantially *richer* if they can convince people that it's true, but it just *isn't* true. Children are still children, and the job of the teacher is still the job of the teacher, although the content may have altered. If I were to ask you the question, 'Does a firefighter need courage?' I would be surprised if anyone sensible suggested otherwise.

So how do you improve as a teacher?

This book has been written with the following assumption: you are a teacher, and you want to get better as a teacher. But rather than provide a million well-meaning 'Here's what you should do if ...' scenarios and tips (for anyone interested in that, see my previous book, *Not Quite a Teacher*, which is a set of stabilizers for the new cyclist). I have invited you to consider what a teacher is, what he or she should be, and what the qualities of that individual might look like.

So how *do* you improve?

This is how:

1. do something
2. reflect on it
3. try something else
4. go back to 2.

And that is as fabulously abstruse as it gets. There is nothing simpler than the structures of our profession; it has been unnecessarily complicated by people who want to sell you something; by people who have something to push; by people peddling ideology and cant. The reality is that in order for us to improve, we have to regress; we have to cut away all the BS and mysticism that has surrounded our profession and return to first principles. Over the next few chapters, I'm going to suggest some techniques that you can practise, or exercises that you can do, that will assist your development as a teacher. Many of them will be things you do already, I hope. Many of them will seem simple; most of them are. Many of them, however, appear easy on the surface, but require determination to carry through and repeat. In other words, they require character, at the same time as they build it.

Aristotle's method of developing character

Aristotle was quite specific about this: in order to develop virtues of the mind, one required instruction, manuals (well, *hello*) and experts who could teach the formal aspects of the virtue being worked. For moral (or character) virtues, such as courage, the technique was simpler, but involved the process described above: practice, reflection, practice, reflection, and so on, and emulating role models. There was no end point; it was meant to be a constant process of educating oneself and sharpening the characteristic under question. One never 'attains' bravery. One never becomes the perfect charmer;[2] it is a process of improvement, reflection and improvement – if you're lucky. Soldiers about to enter war zones for the first time are trained using live ammunition in war games. They have to; they need to feel the fear of hot bullets zipping around their tender mercies in order to prepare them for the real thing, otherwise their courage will liquefy in combat. Far better for it to do so in the playground than the theatre of war.

In the next section of this book, I'll describe some exercises you can do that will help you to improve as a teacher. Like any regime, start slow and build up to bigger weights. At first try some of the exercises that can be done in your head, or at a chair, see how you feel. If you pull something, or feel tempted to soil your immaculate linen, ease off until it doesn't hurt. Never go for the burn, but if you can't feel it, it's probably not helping you. See? I can keep up the sporting metaphors for hours.

Or you can pick exercises that actually terrify you – that probably shows that you recognize some profound weak spot in your repertoire. Go gently into them, and don't expect it to feel perfectly natural. That's the point; unless you can feel a little resistance in your character, it's not challenging you.

I've divided them up into the virtues that they best develop; but of course, real life doesn't fit into boxes (I've tried. Some things do, like shoes, but abstracts are a bugger to pack), and they deliver a workout to several aspects to your character. And because your character is one thing, not a selection of compartments, it ultimately contributes

---

2 Not even Bob Monkhouse.

to the improvement of the whole you. Some people find this kind of challenge terrifying, and never try – remember the teacher who had the same day every day for twenty years? Keep him in mind. But not you – you're choosing to improve yourself.

Trainers on.

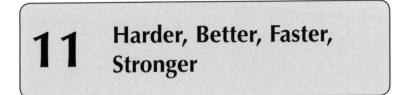

11 Harder, Better, Faster, Stronger

So what do you do now? In the first part of this book I asked you to consider what education was, and what the historical role of the teacher was and is. In the second part I asked you to reflect upon the kind of qualities that you need to focus on in order to be a successful teacher. OK, so what? Does that make you a better professional? Of course not, in the same way that watching a pop concert doesn't make you a better singer, or being able to strip a car engine allows you to take a corner in the Monaco Grand Prix at 150 miles per hour. You have to get out there and do it; if your sleeves aren't rolled up, if you're not in a room with children, if you're not taking kids through years of learning, then you're not going to get better.

There is an enormous debate in education at the moment about how valuable a theoretical grounding is in order to succeed in the profession. Many would claim that because teaching is such a learned craft, time spent in the lecture theatre is pretty much wasted, as it's all theory, and teaching is practical. There is, as with almost any argument, some seed of reason in this. PGCE students can spend as long as they like boning up on Gardner's theory of multiple intelligences, or Maslow's hierarchy of needs, or a million other rentagobs and still be no closer to knowing how to run a room. The eternal fear of the pre-school postgraduate learner is a common one – 'what happens if they misbehave? What do I do?'

But this is a dangerous path; without theory, it is hard to make sense of experience. People have been teaching for thousands of years[1] and only a knucklehead would suggest that there is nothing to be learned from this ocean of experience. And there is another, possibly greater danger – if we relegate the teacher training experience entirely to the school in which they learn, then we condemn all teachers to the vagaries of fate and chance: get a good school and get a good training; luck out (and let's be honest, many will, there are simply far too many teachers needed to be trained for it to be otherwise) and then the best they can hope for is adequate teaching. It also means that teachers will be trained by people, and they will in turn train others, and the process of academic dilution can take place, as the process of inheritance become hostage to the tidemark of the school you learn in. Like homeopathy, eventually all you're left with is bottles of water.[2]

The college experience gives teachers a chance to withdraw from the often manic, panicky experience of the school life, and into an

---

[1] Some of them in the same school.
[2] Sorry, *expensive* bottles of water. Magic ones.

atmosphere where reflection is possible, where sense can be made of all the experiences that have accumulated in the last few months, and sense can be made of it all; where prejudices can be questioned, and advice sought from other professionals, perhaps from a more academic angle, but a questioning, interrogative one nonetheless, rather than the sometimes calcified environment of the classroom, where expediency often trumps innovation, and tradition can often serve as a touchstone for trying something else. Not that there is anything wrong intrinsically with tradition in teaching – and I would argue that an enormous amount of best practice can be found from attending to the reservoir of such tradition – but change and conservatism must be considered simultaneously.

Colleges are often the instruments by which good practice is honed and reinforced, and bad practice withers. And sometimes it isn't – sometimes colleges, particularly if the lecturers and tutors are unwisely gripped by ideology, often hobble students with unnecessary albatrosses of dogma and cant. Well, then schools are the place where this can be challenged, as real life practice takes over the golden utopias of academia. The tension between the two stations is a fundamental part of learning to be a teacher. Becoming a teacher exists in the relationship between these two spaces, not solely in either.

Reflect, experience, reflect

This is the key to becoming a teacher, or *constantly becoming* one, because one can never reach a point where one can say, *I am perfected.* You might always be a teacher as long as you practise, but I use the word 'practise' deliberately. We practise; we get better; we keep trying until the flowers hit the lid. And then we can rest, knowing that we did our part to the best of our ability, and no one can stand against us for it.

So how do you *do*? I'm not asking after your health, but posing a crucial question in order to proceed. What does the concerned teacher do if he/she wants to improve, or to start focusing on the virtues from the start? As Yoda, the renowned educationalist might say, 'Do, or do not. There is no try.' Or as Sean Connery's Bondesque character said to Nicholas Cage in 1998's Oscar-repellent blockbuster *The Rock*, 'Losers always whine about trying their best; winners get to go home and f*ck the Prom Queen.'[3] Which is quite profound. *Do.*

---

[3] Sorry for all the bad swears. My vocabulary is limited.

Perform actions that will reinforce and train the qualities you want to develop.

This is how Aristotle envisaged the training of character, something that we rarely consider these days, or at least rarely in a direct manner. Most often we seem to assume that our characters are stuck the way they are, which is an oddly deterministic approach to take, because it implies that we have no free will, no ability to change ourselves as people. Perhaps this is because changing your character is such an abstract process, invisible to the eye, naked or augmented. Or perhaps we have succumbed to the mental malaise that suggests that all human action is the product of forces beyond our control – genetics, upbringing and socialization – and that we have no influence over something so abstract as character. Or worse, perhaps we now exist in a continuum where the very idea that our characters *need* changing can't be considered. This romantic idea of the individual, and its intrinsic value, is an abyss of narcissism and nihilism.

Character *can* be changed, honed and improved – or ruined; the pendulum swings both ways. The greatest part of the education is carried out in our infancy, when the broad brushstrokes of our character are formed, some say in formative months, but certainly years. But that isn't the end of our evolution as people – of course it isn't. Your character changes throughout your life, whether you will it or not. So what supplies the fuel for this engine of change?

Experience. The things we see, hear, feel and with every other sensual apparatus absorb become part of who we are. If we are treated roughly, we often succumb to the vice of roughness; tortured children can toughen, break or be scarred forever – the effects are as personal as a fingerprint, but effects there are. One of the more beautiful aspects of human nature is that the same experience can affect people in unique ways, defying the attempts of social science to restrict our behaviour and psychology to easily predicted packets of prognostication. That said, there are points where human character is, if not concrete, at least level and constant – if it were not so, then there would be nothing predictable about people at all. Yet we do say, with some degree of accuracy, 'He's a brave man,' or 'She's a kind woman,' and know what it means, and what it describes. It speaks of regularities in human characters that might not be inescapable articles of certainty or demonstrable natural laws of motion, but are good rules-of-thumb.

Character can be changed. You can change it, and experiences are the key to this. If some experiences develop us this way, and others shape our characters in another, how can we use this to change the way we operate in our professional roles?

Aiming for experiences that will change us

By aiming for experiences that will provide us with opportunities to improve the virtues we have decided we wish to improve. By realizing that the experiences we stumble through affect our character in various ways, so we should decide and select our experiences with as much deliberation as we do (or perhaps don't) select our diet, or our friends, or the movie you want to watch tonight. With care.[4]

The second aspect of this process is choosing. Choosing, or deciding, is a product of willpower, and there is no tried and tested way of developing this. Do, or do not. There is no try, remember. Just select the things you wish to do, and then do them; if you lack the willpower to do this, then no amount of inspirational manuals will be able to help you do otherwise.

But I invite you to consider the stakes in this game – drift along as the product of your environment and pretend that you are the master of your destiny? Or make choices that define you, and develop you into the shape you wish to be, as if *you* were the potter of your own character rather than a lump of clay on a wheel. There's a healthy dose of existentialism in this philosophy, for those who care to lift up the stone and look underneath. You'll find references at the back. If you choose to look …

Nobody can – unless you are truly coerced – make you do anything you really don't want to do. Any action you make is, tacitly or otherwise, approved by you. In many ways, there is a useful comparison to be made between character-forming and body-building. Unless you are restrained by disability, you get the body you choose. KFC, nights in white satin and taxis everywhere? Hello, Muu-muu. Bottles of water, early nights and breaking a sweat every now and then. Hello, ladies. It's not nuclear physics. You are not helpless. You have an enormous amount of influence over the life you want, which I know sounds a bit Anthony Robbins, but unlike any number of rictus-faced gurus, I'm not selling you anything you can't learn in five minutes of reflection. I merely wish to point out what is

---

[4] *The Twelve Men of Christmas* is a particularly chilling mistake to make, incidentally. Be warned.

so obvious that we barely notice it, like the clouds scudding along: there is no fate but the one we make.

Of course, we aren't gods; we don't dictate the motion of anything other than our own poor selves, and it is an illusion to pretend otherwise; the only thing you control is you. So it stands to reason that we should do things within our dominion (i.e. you, again) that make us happier, more fulfilled and flourish, however we define it. If I am unhappy with my emergent beer-gut and the difficulty I find rising from a Lazyboy,[5] then I get on a bike and do a few laps. I choose to do with myself as I wish. And after this project, I might find that, although I still cannot control anything other than myself, I have opened opportunities to myself that were previously unavailable; the benefits of a bike body, the sense of well-being, increased attractiveness to others, etc.

So, too, with character. You may whine to others, 'Oh, I'd love to do that, but I'm not brave enough', as if bravery were anything other than the description we give to someone who does something others would consider brave. Bravery isn't a magic property one possesses; it's a habit, an inclination to act in a certain way. Unless someone has strapped you to the chair, you can be it any time you want.

Example: I used to be terrified of heights. I'm not sure if this is a phobia or not, although it has a Latin name and everything, because it is, I think, perfectly justifiable to be terrified of heights. Unlike open spaces or small spiders, they ARE fatal, so I would say that it was a justifiable fear. Anyway. I was once asked if I would participate in a tandem parachute jump for charity. Of course, my viscera turned into a cement mixer at the thought of it, and I knew, I *knew* that I wouldn't be able to do it, because even the thought of being at the top of a set of ladders reduced me to tapioca.

So I said yes.

Not because I'm trying to appear Billy Big-Balls, because believe me, I'm not.[6] But because I knew, in exactly the same way I knew that stepping off the platform in the leap of faith was impossible, that it was simply a question of a series of decisions. The first step was to say yes. That was easy enough, I can say yes to order. I'm an expert at it, I should win prizes. Saying yes wasn't hard at all. The next step was collecting money; that's also a bit of a fear of mine, as I have a pathological tendency to be embarrassed when asking anyone for money (although my parents may disagree). But again, nothing too

---

[5] The chair, not the...oh *you.*
[6] Don't ask me how I know.

bad. The next step was to tell others; then, to turn up for the taxi. Then, to go along on a sunny morning to the airfield, and finally to don the outlandish jumpsuit and listen to the instructions.

Next I had to walk to a plane – on the ground, which is safe, you see – and then climb in – and literally on – to the lap of a big ex-army guy. You have never experienced social discomfort until you have sat in a plane in the lap of a strange man trying to make small talk. Ten thousand feet later, and with my legs dangling out of the side of a plane, with nothing but Berkshire below me, I felt a strange sense of calm; dozens of tiny steps had brought me here, dozens of small decisions.

One big step later and I was on the ground, fist pumping and doing a curious little victory dance that I'm glad was off camera.

Incidentally, I have never felt scared of heights since. Oh, standing at the top of the Empire State will make your saddle do funny things, to be sure, but it's never the same again. I was much higher, much, much higher, you see, and I didn't die. And my body knows this. It kind of shrugs at it and goes, 'Call that high? Ha.' It was a way of acclimatizing myself to that experience. I would do it again in a heartbeat, and feel only a tiny amount of the anticipation of before, because it has gone from an unknown to a known. It has entered my intellectual and emotional repertoire as an experience with depth, complexity and meaning. It has been absorbed into me.

In this section I will suggest experiences that you can choose, as a teacher, to create and absorb. Some of them will require nothing more than time and patience. Some of them will require resources, or the agreement of others. Some of them are so easy you can do them in a locked box, and others are difficult, and require you to rise to the occasion in such a manner that implies you are being sent on a secret mission to kill Hitler. I have divided them up into the relevant sections/virtues that we have discussed, and left a section at the end for other, more general exercises that you can do. Some of them will not be applicable in your school, and others will make you suspect I'm watching your life on a webcam.[7]

Good luck.

---

[7] I'm not. Probably.

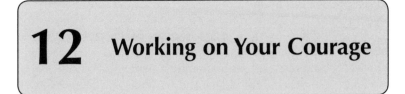

12 Working on Your Courage

SPARTAN RISK ASSESSMENT

To achieve greater courage in the classroom, do things that require it; deliberately put yourself in situations where *not* to have courage would make things difficult, or untenable. Often merely the act of putting yourself forward for a fearful act is enough to be able to claim that you have exercised courage. Whatever you choose to do, remember that courage is not the sensation of never feeling fear; it is the action of doing what one is afraid of, despite how fast your heart is beating.

Make a phone call home
Call a parent and speak to them for five minutes about their child, your pupil. Often the fear of speaking to strangers is enough to paralyze some, although this is a strange fear indeed for a teacher to have. Most, almost all parents in my experience are amenable to a friendly, professional call home, and will welcome some feedback as to how X is doing. To make it even easier, start off by making some calls to parents of children who have been doing really well or working hard, and deserve a little home praise. Not only do you improve the classroom relationship, but the parent associates you and the school with good news – everyone's a winner. Trust me, you'll feel fabulous, and so will everyone else.

Once you've done that, move on to a more difficult call – perhaps it's a parent you've been putting off, because you have bad news. Or perhaps it's a parent that has a reputation for giving – but taking no – sh*t. Whatever. Make it easier on yourself by speaking in a calm, respectful manner, and start the conversation with something positive: 'Little Jimmy is normally great in my lessons – but he's been letting himself down a bit and I need your help getting him back on track ….' etc. That should take the heat out of most conversations, and even give you some emotional leverage with them.

The beautiful thing is, once you've done this a few times, and had successful results, the fear of making calls will melt away, and eventually you feel neutral towards them, and possibly even eventually positive. Might take a while though ….

Take a whole school assembly
I can hear people running out of the door already. Yes, speaking to the whole school sounds like the most manic piece of aversion therapy that anyone can suggest ('Scared of spiders? How about we eat one!' etc). But this is one of the harder exercises in courage pumping that you can do at school, short of challenging the entire sixth form to a simultaneous cage fight,[1] and produces some of the biggest rewards. The chance to talk to the whole school at once in a formal setting is invaluable; you raise your profile with children who might otherwise not know you; you get to talk about something that burns a hole in your soul, and share it with others; and with luck you might get something important across to the kids. Who knows? Whatever you choose to talk about, try to make it something positive, something that they can understand (although it doesn't have to be from within

---

[1] Beef! etc.

their immediate life experiences; it's a great opportunity to challenge their preconceptions, and to educate them in many ways). If you choose to do 'what I did on my holidays', then make sure your holidays were spectacularly exciting.

Once you have taken an assembly, and seen a hundred, a thousand pairs of eyes on you, the experience is often intoxicating; terrifying but intoxicating. And in the manner of a good karaoke session, you'll get the bug, and if it goes well, as soon as you leave the stage you'll think to yourself, *again, again*. If you persist with this, it can become addictive, especially if you pace yourself to, say, a monthly session, by which point you'll have thought of a good theme to explore. For some teachers, the requirement to produce an assembly every week (sometimes more) drives them into the ground with boredom like a tent peg, and inspiration can often prove hard to find. But by God, you won't be scared anymore.

Ask someone to observe your lesson

Some teachers spend a lifetime trying to avoid being observed. Why on earth would you encourage it? Because if *you* ask to be observed, then you can set the boundaries, and ask to be observed for a specific aspect that you want to improve. Or, if you're feeling braver, just ask them to do a general observation and throw caution to the wind. Teaching is a profession, and the best people to evaluate it are professionals; ones that you admire and respect; ones who are prepared to give up their time and evaluate you, and give you tips and pointers about where to go next. Your professional development doesn't stop when you get the certificate saying you're a teacher. It continues as long as you teach ... if you let it.

As it's an informal observation, you needn't worry about it being set against your record in any way – it's for *your* benefit, not for some plodding administrative paper exercise. And rather than simply taking the observer you're given – often an external assessor who doesn't know the context of the class – you can choose someone who knows the pupils; or better, also teaches them. And for extra heart-pumping thrills, you could ask someone who teaches in a different style, or even, if you wish, someone who is the polar opposite to your teaching. Why the hell not? Every teacher has their own style, and we can often learn the most from people that we normally would disagree with.

Get feedback from other people at school

I'm going to say this very carefully, because it's such a minefield I can barely write about it without tiptoeing and holding my breath.

You could get feedback from the kids.

WARNING. This is not some pointless, hellish sop to student voice, the moronic campaign of disempowering the classroom teacher because someone in the DfE read a book by Montessori and thought, *aren't children lovely? Let's put them in charge.* Because make no mistake, student voice, taken to any length, is the death of the teacher's authority. But ..... the children can act as a reservoir of information that can be useful to access *if* you go about it carefully, and make it clear that you are in the driving seat of the process.

I have in my career held back some of the kids whom you know you can trust, the ones who exhibit unusual levels of maturity, the ones who have hearts that were apparently crafted by little elves in Santa's factory. These are the ones that you can often get some great info from – and at times I have. I asked them, 'What can I do to get the naughty kids behaving?' (this was in the early years), and the answer was invariably to the point and focused on what seems to matter to the child. Of course, you have to be prepared to hear some home truths too, but at the same time you should take everything they say in context – they are, after all children, and just because their perspective is privileged, it doesn't mean that they are necessarily correct. Children are just as capable of making mistakes about their own evaluations, never forget. They are not the fairy fountain of truth, as some educationalists seem to suggest because they've heard too many Whitney Houston songs.

Organize a trip

Trips are great. They are also an enormous pain in the ass. They are both. They are also very, very rewarding, and exhausting. They are many things, but they are, if done properly, also an eye-opener. There are few things as effective for developing relationships between yourself and your students as a well-planned and well-executed trip, because you become a different person on these occasions than merely the hard-ass in the corner who gives them a hard time – you become the one who looks after them, and for many children that is a powerful association to make. This is a great responsibility, and there is a great pay-off afterwards.

But, you may ask yourself, can I do this? Can I plan it properly? The answer is yes, you can *nods to Obama*. I suggest you don't start off with taking entire year groups free-climbing up the Old Man of Hoy;[2] begin with a target group, on a local trip somewhere interesting. If

---

[2] However you choose to interpret this.

you don't live anywhere interesting then find something interesting about it – I knew a teacher who organized a nature trail on the high street of a big town; but she was great at seeing things with a different lens from everyone else.

Make a list

How does this entail or exercise bravery? What I mean is for you to face up to all the jobs that are mewling, screaming, crying out to be done, and you've filed them on a million post-it notes and forget-me memos at the bottom of your bag, or worse, in your head. I feel your pain; I am you. But this is no way to proceed as an adult and a professional, and I would say that around two-thirds of the teachers I have known work like this. So step up, make a list of EVERTHING on your plate, and be brave enough to confront the tasks you *have* to do rather than hope that if you ignore them long enough they'll wither away. Some will; others turn toxic, and a problem ignored often takes root, and turns from a weed to a beanstalk.

And when you have everything written down on the list, you will notice differences between them; some of the tasks are titans; some are tiny tittles. Some could be done in a heartbeat; some will take months. Some have to be done, some need to be done, and some would just be nice. Some are for you, some are for others, and some are for line managers. Some are important; some are not. Break them down into *must* do's and *might* do's, and tick them off on a daily basis. Carry any over that you haven't completed. Organize them by deadlines, so that you can spread them over your available time. See what you've done? You've tamed your life. And now, perhaps the voices will stop …

Of course, there might be some jobs that can't be tamed, no matter how organized you get. In that case, the next task you can try is …

Say NO

This syllable apparently terrifies some people. I know; it used to terrify me. 'Tom, can you come along on a trip to Alton Towers and look after the EBD kids?'; 'Tom, can you lead an INSET on EAL phonics?'; 'Tom, can you take my Saturday detentions for the next month?'; 'Tom, can you pick up an extra class every week please?'; 'Tom, can you move the staff room three inches to the left please?'

You will be assailed by the tiresome antics of others, who look at you and, in the manner of a hungry man in a Bugs Bunny cartoon, will hallucinate that you are some kind of prize turkey. 'Oh boy, Tom looks like he's got five minutes spare. Let's clobber him with something.' There are people whose sole aim is to give you things to do. Often these things are Very Important To Them, and Not Very Important To You.

So learn to say *no* to people. This isn't rude; but learn to resist simply saying yes to everyone when they ask for help. This might be because you are a lovely person who bleeds the milk of human kindness. It may be because you are a broken spirit and no one respects you – you be the judge. But the more you say *yes* to things, the more people will ask you; you become the go-to guy whenever someone's in a pickle. That would be great, but you have stuff to do too, I presume, and you will NEVER, I say NEVER[3] get them done if you're spending half your time helping others to achieve their aims. When you get asked to help out, consider if you really have to do it, if you want to do it, if you see value in it and, most of all, why aren't *they* bloody doing it? If someone just wants to make their own lives easier, then tell them to stick it up their plenary. If it's a box-ticking exercise to make them look good, say no and laugh at them as you do, wiping tears from your eyes, and saying,' Oh that's bloody priceless, thanks I needed that....oh wait, you're SERIOUS?!' before launching off into another fit. They'll get the message.

Saying no to people is hard; it requires ninja levels of front simply to look at someone and say, 'No, I won't help you,' before sucking on your pipe and looking out the window. Far better (and more polite) to say that you're too busy. And it's probably true. Every week I allocate an afternoon, or a few free lessons[4] for *myself*, because I know there will be letters to write, observations to write up, and random tasks that need to be completed. I *know* this. So when someone asks if I can help move a room full of textbooks or something, I say, 'Sorry, I've got a meeting.' I do – a meeting with myself. We're dreadfully embarrassed about saying that we've saved some time for ourselves. But these are the kinds of things we need to plan for in order to get things done. Don't be shy about scheduling time for *your* jobs. That's how you achieve things. And if anyone says, 'Oh, but I thought you were free at that time,' then you have my permission to chin them for their oafish temerity.

Don't be the Yes-Man; be the No-Man. Try it. It's intoxicating. You will feel a surge of power that is practically indecent. And bizarrely enough, people will actually respect you more for it. How about that?

---

[3] Copyright Foghorn Leghorn.
[4] Often referred to as non-contact time, but I don't call lessons 'contact time' so I don't see the link.

Do a public duty

Most schools get their teaching staff involved in break/ lunch/ pre-post-school crowd control, monitoring areas, corridors, play areas, etc. If you don't have one, and you've got some spare time (did I just say that?) then you should. They don't last long, and it gets your face known around school – otherwise you can become 'that weird guy in the corridor'. At least this way you start getting to know names of students that you would otherwise miss, no matter how much you want to.

Change the seating plan

Most classrooms benefit from a seating plan that reinforces your dominance over the space, assists with names, and ensures that social grouping doesn't unwittingly interrupt education. If you don't have one, you probably should – and don't wait until the next term or half term to do so (the common cop-out, the teacher equivalent of hitting the snooze button). Start it next lesson. One reason why many teachers don't do this (especially if they have been teaching a group for a while) is that 'the kids will moan/kick off if I attempt to regroup them.' So what? It's your room. They will resist, but their resistance isn't the important issue at stake – that accolade belongs to their education. Your room, your rules.

Reboot the class rules

If you're wise (and I'm sure you are) then you'll have made your behaviour expectations clear to them from the very first day you met them. Your boundaries may be broad or narrow, but you must have them, and the kids must know that they exist. As Bill Rogers says, the certainty of the sanction is more important than the severity, which I also believe. But even the best of classroom relationships can benefit from touching base with those regulations from time to time – and if your class relationships are anything less than perfect (imagine that) then you will definitely need to do this: reboot.

There isn't a button you can press that serves this function – you are the button. Next lesson you have, start them off with a quiet but sincere reminder of the rules that you have in the room, why you have them, and the consequences/rewards for crossing or observing them. Even with my very best classes, I have to reboot occasionally during the lesson; gather all their attention, and remind them why you've stopped the lesson and so on. Children, even the loveliest of them, can forget themselves, and by returning to the basics from time to time, you reassure and reinforce the best ways that they learn, for their and your benefit. It takes a bit of grit to do this with some classes. Pick one that needs to hear about boundaries and do it tomorrow.

How's my teaching?

Similar to observations, why not arrange to meet someone you respect, and whom you trust to be honest and professional, and ask them to give you an informal appraisal of your teaching, not just in the classroom, but around school in general. This isn't part of the scheduled observation cycles, just an honest opinion honestly sought. You might be surprised at the kinds of things that come up. Pick your partner carefully – make sure it's someone who has your interests at heart. Does your mum work at your school?

Learn something new

If you have any degree of self-awareness, you'll know what you're good at, and what you could be better at. Instead of doing what most of us do, which is to ignore that flaw, or think it isn't important, why not face up to it, and decide to do something about it? If you feel a bit weak on nineteenth-century land reform (and you're not a PE teacher) then tackle the lack yourself; find out. Enrol on a course; sign up for an INSET; attend an adult education college; work towards a masters; anything that tackles a soft spot that you would like to harden.[5]

Walk a mile in someone else's shoes

Think you've got it bad? Next time you have some free time, walk through the school until you see a supply teacher, or a new teacher, or just any teacher who is obviously struggling with some students. Walk in and offer to take a pupil out with you, or summon another teacher, or get supplies, or anything that they might need. In schools where colleagues do this for each other, consistently, problems melt away. In schools where teachers barricade themselves into classrooms like medieval castles, they find that one is the loneliest number. See: *siege mentality*. It takes guts, and effort to do this for someone else; they will never forget it, if your help is honestly and deliberately meant. For God's sake, don't offer to help and then make a face if they say they need it. Yes, you'll lose some time. It's worth it.

---

[5] That came out wrong.

Don't let something go

We all develop blind spots; things that once we used to confront, but now we've learned to live with. Well, maybe we shouldn't. Do the kids all pile into your lesson in the manner of the Abyssinian hordes? Do you remember when that used to bug you? Think harder, and get bugged again. It could be a uniform infringement, it could be late homework, it could be lack of effort, it could be a million things that you – and perhaps others – now let slide on the assumption that it's someone else's job,. It probably isn't; it's almost always everyone's job. Behaviour and effort is everyone's responsibility; you, by definition are part of everyone. Pick one thing that you won't bend on for a day, and then don't.

Introduce yourself to someone you don't know at school

Yes, I'm aware that this has a high chance of making you look a bit mental; try to be subtle; but find someone that you don't normally work with and ask them what they do, and tell them what you do. It amazes me how many auxiliary and support staff go unnoticed in schools by teaching practitioners – yet these are the people who make our jobs possible. So say hello to the janitor, the cleaner, the admin, the boy Friday ... whoever makes life possible for you. I guarantee that at some point, you will value making the relationship. It is also, I might add, superlative manners.

Try teaching in a different style from the one you normally have

You know exactly what I'm talking about. We all develop a groove that we slide into without thinking. For me, it's the lecture; I can bang on for hours about my favourite subjects and themes. Now, that's appropriate at times, but I know that it's not the last word in sixth-form education, so I have to deliberately restrain myself and make myself set group tasks and research, when appropriate. Sometimes it's painful. You will know your own default (which as a child I noticed was 'textbook and questions' for most of my teachers). So do something that you don't normally do – I'm not suggesting that you try any old, witless, pointless innovation for its own sake. But break out of your comfort zone a little, and give it your heart for a lesson or two. Don't half-try something new and then say, 'Ah, see that was rubbish,' just because you didn't try it properly. Really try something new. Maybe it IS rubbish. But you won't know until you find out.

Quit

Didn't see that coming did you? It's true. The biggest complacency we can fall into is immobility. Are you happy with your job? Does it look like it's getting better? Are there opportunities for you? Do you like working there? Does the school ethos suit you? Is it falling apart?

Maybe you should move on. Many people are happy to settle, but I guarantee you that if you settle like this for more than a few years, you'll calcify, unless your tolerance of boredom is extremely high, or you teach maths (ho-ho). Moving on is often the biggest adventure you can face. Are you ready?

Move sideways

The baby brother of quitting. Ask for a new role; apply for a position, or even better, apply for a position that doesn't exist (and I don't mean something stupid like Head of Time Travel. I mean a role that you think the school needs but doesn't have … yet'. I worked with Louisa, a brilliant teacher who wanted to start up the Duke of Edinburgh scheme. There was no money for it, so it was entirely self-financed. It went so well that four years later it's a paid post, on every prospectus and website we have, and is a key part of our extension program in Upper School. Some challenges pay off.

Or you could just try to break into something else at school that already exists. There are bound to be plenty of activities that could use a spare pair of hands in an after-school club, or some admin, or even just a body. There are also an enormous number of roles inside school that you could branch into.

CRITICAL THINKING SKILLS

'THANK YOU FOR THE CAREFUL PLANNING, DIFFERENTIATION, RESOURCES, GROUP WORK, INDEPENDENT LEARNING & PACE. WE HATE YOU.'

This is a difficult virtue to improve, for the simple reason that patience normally involves the absence of activity and the forbearance of action. That's not to say that it doesn't involve doing anything; the absence of action is not itself inactivity. The decision to forbear is an action in itself, and patience could be described as a series of decisions *not* to do something, like the chain-smoker sweating as he watches an episode of Mad Men or an old noir film. Here are some activities that you can do that require you to be patient, and by that process practise the art of restraint.

Set a detention – and mean it

This sounds like an obvious one. But an enormous number of perfectly reasonable teachers suffer from the problem of issuing a time-based sanction for some transgression, and then, when the moment occurs, they reduce the sanction to a matter of moments because their hearts have softened or, more likely, because by the time it gets to the end of a long day they feel shattered, and can't face the misery of detaining themselves let alone anyone else. This is perfectly understandable, and I certainly don't want to suggest that a teacher doesn't have the right to amend his or her decisions.

But to suffer some classroom misdemeanour or worse, and then to reduce the sentence simply because 'Aww, it's four o'clock, let's hit the trail,' is to make a mockery of the system you've put in place to deter bad behaviour. So keep strong; if you say half an hour, then *mean* half an hour, and grit your teeth and sit it out. Letting pupils earn it off (i.e. work their detention down by means of good behaviour) is another way of telling students that it's OK to disrupt education, as long as you make a sad face and do the right thing afterwards. Surely the expectation is that pupils *don't misbehave at all*; anything less is to reward (and therefore encourage) misbehaviour. It feels weird – that's the problem – but for some people the simplest way to work on their patience is to do what they say they will.

When you start a project/experiment/program with your kids/department/faculty, set a deadline

You can guess the next part: 'and stick to it.' It takes time for projects to work; sometimes the time they need exceeds what you originally envisaged. Kids don't suddenly make quantum leaps in their education – any programme or intervention you design is going to be like steering a large ship across the ocean. So whenever you begin something, set a deadline, or a minimum amount of time you'll allow for something to take root. And even if things don't seem to be working at first, keep focused on the deadline you set. Of course, if the project is obviously going down like a kite made of uranium, and for reasons that are obviously clear, then you know when you have to cancel. But try not to lose your nerve (there's courage again) and hold fast.

Let the children work independently

This is a good activity (and an especially hard one) if you are a control freak, and don't feel comfortable with a lesson unless you are doing something for every second of it. These are the teachers (and I've been guilty in my innocent past) who feel they have to be talking, or directing, or moving around, or demonstrating, or pointing, or clicking, or … just about anything, as if the harder *you* work, the better they learn. Don't mistake me – a teacher should be doing quite a lot; but you can't learn for them. They have to be doing things too – I understand the fashionable ratio of teacher input: student activity is 1:5 or something like that. Whatever it is, it's a good general principle.

So set some work that requires the students to be working by themselves with minimal interaction from you (minimum, not none; you always need to be available, and some need you to be more available than others). I used to have to grind my teeth and nail my hands to the desk to prevent me from bouncing back up and shouting, 'OK, let's move on!' Pace is a great thing, but sometimes the right pace is a slow one, depending on the class, activity and topic. So chill out, and let them do the work for a change.

The best way to do this is, again, to set a deadline, and stick to it; let any pupil who has a watch be amazed as you constantly and consistently meet the agreed time target. It also helps them to trust you; you mean what you say. So give a task a time boundary, and let them work right up to that point.

Plant something

You heard me. There are no short cuts in gardening, only the right thing to do and the wrong thing to do. And sometimes the right thing to do, as in life, is nothing. There are few activities so metaphorically demonstrative of this principle as growing something. If you're a primary teacher, this is an easy one to integrate into your lessons; the class can start a nature table, or look after a patch of the school ground, or you can put a bloody sunflower pot on your desk. In secondary, there are often fewer opportunities, unless you're working on an appropriate geography/science project. But you can still do this for your own pleasure, or in your own work space.

Growing a plant or flower is maddeningly slow; if you really struggle with this kind of thing, then you might want to start with bamboo or some similarly fecund vegetable before you move on to bonsai. But there is nothing as powerful to demonstrate the Power of Slow as tending something living, and watching it grow. Not unlike children, I might add.

Reflect on how your students have turned out
If you have a few years' experience with the same students and classes, or if you have knowledge of their fates after they have left your care, you could do a lot worse than mentally map the progress that they have made. Pick five students at random; ask yourself what you first thought of them when you met – were they swots or clots? Then ask yourself how they turned out after a few weeks, a few months a few years. How many of them confirmed your initial impressions? How many of them challenged them? How many blew them away? Gaining an ability to see a pupil as a product of years not lessons is a powerful way to realize that, like plants, people measure their lives not in heartbeats, but in seasons, and longer. You should do the same. Sometimes it takes time for a child to mature, to realize, to become the person you think they can be.

Take time to consider how YOU have developed
This is also a good exercise if you have a few years experience under your cardigan. What kind of teacher were you when you began? What kind of teacher are you now? If you're of an analytical bent you could score yourself for a variety of attributes: happy; well-organized; fulfilled; challenged; optimistic, and so on. It sounds mindless, but it's a clean way of telling, albeit skewed by your own perceptions (but then this is a task all about perceptions and relative esteem) how you have changed.

Gaining a sense of how you change is an enormously powerful way of recognizing who we are, and identifying the unifying concept that ties You (five years ago) to You (now). The unifying concept, incidentally, is You. Gaining a sense of the river flowing can be very helpful in understanding how the passage of time changes things, and sometimes how the most apparently immutable of things (your dearly held beliefs, your attitudes) can soften, harden or bend as years go by.

One lesson this teaches us, or can teach us, is that true change often takes time. It is as true of us as it is of others. If you look at your mirror every day, you barely notice a change; but look at a picture of yourself ten years ago, and you'll be amazed at the differences rather than similarities. You never *see* your hair grow, but there it is, long and dandy at the back and badly in need of some barbershop love. If you want to change, and if you want to help others change, it's going to take time. And taking time requires patience.

Do something else

This is a bit philosophical. One of the best ways to avert the sense of frustration and impatience that often accompanies our waiting is to divert or distract our attention from the thing being waited for. If you're engaged in a task that requires you to be patient, then for God's sake don't make waiting the task, otherwise all you'll be able to think about is the excruciating dissonance between the state you're in and the state you're waiting for. The aphoristic watched kettle will boil, to be sure, but you will drive yourself insane as you wait, pretending that you have some kind of telepathic power that can will it to boil more quickly (we've all been there). The whole principle of Chinese water torture is based on this quality of our impatience; that anticipation can often lead us into the irreparable realms of intolerance and insanity. Try waiting for a child to remove a set of headphones, and you'll know what torture is all about.

So if you're in a position where you simply need to wait and do nothing, then do something else, unrelated to the activity. If you're waiting for chewing gum to be removed from the oily crevice of some lad's mouth, then as you're doing it, resolve some other issue with another student, or check on someone's work (with half an eye open for the actions of the chewing-gum kid). That way you don't over-focus on the thing you're waiting for, and risk falling into the 'I must do something' trap that such situations often provoke.

Bite your tongue

John Travolta in *Get Shorty* uttered a line that immortalized itself. When his partner – a gangster – was worried about what he would say in a tight spot, he simply replied, 'I'm going to say as little as necessary.' He paused. 'If that.'

It's the last bit that I like. The idea that more words = better communication is a demonstrably fallible principle; yet so often we spoil the impact of what we want to convey by surrounding the important message with lesser ones. Instead of rushing over to children who are misbehaving, shouting the odds, walk slowly up to them, and instead of launching into one, pause, and then simply say. 'Jack, outside. The rest of you, get on with your work.' Very little more than that needs be said on some occasions – you will be the judge. But framing your sentences with as much empty air as possible will lend your words a frame that conveys gravity and seriousness; it invites people to consider your words with the solemnity they deserve – as long as you sound like you mean it.

TEACHER PRESENCE

'THESE AREN'T THE GRADES I'M LOOKING FOR.'

Fill in your planner properly (organization)
I don't know any teacher who operates at maximum effectiveness without recourse to a diary; yet many teachers struggle along with

the novel ambition of remembering everything they need in their heads. And when I say 'remembering' what I actually mean, of course, is 'not remembering', which is exactly what happens. Buying a planner and putting all your relevant details in one place is one of the best time investments you will ever make. Everyone you ever phone, every appointment and deadline you make (and then meet), all the behaviour issues, sanctions, rewards, all the homework set, missed and handed in … it all goes in one place and you will escape 'Oh my God is that today?' hell. And people will think that you're a genius. Seriously, it's like the monkeys in *2001: A Space Odyssey*, they'll practically worship you.

USE your planner every day (organization)

Having a planner with lots of numbers in it is just dandy; but it becomes a useless tool if you do nothing with it. Get into the habit of looking at it at least twice a day: once at the start of the day to remind yourself what steam you need to get together for that day, and once at the end of the day so you can record anything you need to follow up, or where you need to be the next day. This is one of the most valuable habits you can ever acquire in such an incessant, unpredictable, yet simultaneously predictable environment.

Send a positive letter home (compassion/justice)

We can get so tangled up with poor behaviour and punishment that we often lose sight of the good things that happen. This is dangerous for two reasons; one, because it misses an essential part of behaviour management and pupil relationships – reinforcing desired behaviour by rewarding the righteous – and also because it helps us form the false impression that there is nothing to the children other than poor behaviour, which is almost always patent nonsense. We are so keenly attuned to misbehaviour that we often completely forget that the majority of kids are probably doing what you want them to do for the majority of the time. So sit down, and force yourself to think of, say, three kids who, in your opinion, deserve some home praise. Things like that stay with kids for a long, long time, and as an act of kindness, there's a hell of a lot of benefit in it for you too.

Clear out your in-tray (organization)

If you are human, you will probably have a number of areas reserved for work in progress – a desk, an in-tray, a pigeonhole, a locker, an office, depending on how high up the food chain you are. Today, be honest with yourself; what do I have in my in-tray that I will never,

ever do? Perhaps it's the pamphlets for Machu Picchu that you keep meaning to organize, or the invitation to attend an INSET on Finnish that you think might make great CPD. Sometimes you just have to accept that you will never do these things, in which case, stop cluttering up your eye line with them and creating a pile of unrealistic never-never tasks that simply make you feel rubbish. You only have 24 hours in the day. If you haven't done it after a few months, you probably aren't in the right place to do so. So get rid.

Move jobs from the in-tray to the long-term store (organization)
There may still be things that you aren't going to do ..... not this year anyway. Again, be honest, and move them somewhere you can access, but not somewhere that will interrupt how you work. There are few things more futile than trying to find the sheet of paper with a parent's phone number on it (important) under a stack of brochures for midnight mystery walks in Whitechapel and never-to-be-used lesson plans.

Sort out your cupboard (organization)
If you are fortunate enough to have a dedicated storage area for your department, then streamlining this area can make a small but constant difference to the way you work. A simple set of rules of thumb that your grandmother probably told you, so I'll repeat, are these:

1.   If you don't use it, or love it, then throw it out.
2.   If you haven't touched it in two years, then you don't use it. Stop pretending it's useful.
3.   If you use it, put it at a convenient height, and close to the front of the space. If it's storage, then put it up high, where you'll never need it. As you reorganize your cupboard, there should be a tidal process of objects and resources drifting upwards, as if unto Heaven. When it exceeds the top shelves/back areas, then you can safely send it to recycling Heaven.

Film yourself[1] (courage)
This takes some stones. Borrow a movie camera and organize someone to film you during part of a lesson. It's perfectly legal, and absolutely without controversy, despite what some may say, as long as you use it for personal training only, you don't upload it anywhere

---

[1]   NOT like that. Do you think about Christmas with that mind?

public, and you don't allow it to be used for career progression or disciplinary purposes. It is best, anyway, if it is trained on you, so normally there will only be a sea of backs of heads to contend with. This task is an absolute eye-opener. It is awesome watching yourself, and often not in a good way. Your pelvic saddle will do something peculiar as you see what you look like to others. A great way to temper some of your more obvious body-language faux pas. Robert Burns once wrote, 'Oh wad some power the giftie gie us To see oursels as ithers see us!'[2] Well, now you can.

Shadow another colleague (compassion)

I don't mean anonymously[3]. Spend a day, a half-day, a few free hours, following a class, a colleague or a student. Remember, like you did in your training (if you followed a college-/ uni-based course)? It's even more powerful once you've been teaching for some time, because by this point you know what you're looking for. Have a focus that you can stick to, or keep your lens wide and watch for it all, going for broad empirical understanding rather than anything too neat: up to you. You can also think about swapping lessons with another colleague for a session/day or two. If you're reasonably well-known around school, it isn't like supply anymore, it's a real eye-opener, especially if you follow through and try to teach their subject. A genuine pick-you-up-and-wake-you-up.

Write an essay on teaching (analysis/wisdom)

Yeah, I know, you're kidding me, right? I certainly am not. As trainee teachers we are often compelled, for fear of failure, to research and create original (or at least self-generated) essays and features on an educational topic. While few of us enjoy sweating without purpose, these activities do serve an end; they formalize and structure our attitude and understanding of education and teaching. It's a mistake to think that all formal training ends as soon as you throw your mortarboard in the air. And far too many teachers think that they'll never look at another teacher-training manual as long as they live. Which is sad, because there is an enormous amount – and I'm talking Leviathan quantities – of data, research, advocacy and opinion out there written by our professional predecessors.

Why not dip your toe in and research something that you're interested in – more able students, working with EAL kids, the

---

[2] He spoke like this a lot.
[3] We've all been there.

history of education? Because there's no pressure to produce this, the motivation will have to come from within. But the removal of a formal deadline or focus means that you can write it as you like, when you like. The freedom is terrifying. Of course you can learn about anything you want; the internet is free, and full of data; the libraries are too (remember them? They're like *Idea Stores*, only with books, silence and no game zones).

If you want to take this to career-enhancing heights, then you could ask to present it at the next staff meeting, INSET or whatever, as a way of sharing the information you gathered. You swot.

Formally train towards something (wisdom/knowledge)

As a teacher you probably have some kind of continuing professional training entitlement from your school, which means they allocate finance and time for you to train in some way. Normally most teachers spend their chips on externally run INSETs; these are of variable quality (and I should know; I provide some with the TES) and some are very ropey indeed, as some geriatric chancer who couldn't hack it in a modern classroom attempts to tell you how to 'inspire' the kids.[4] I once attended an INSET on catering for the more able student; we ran through some fabulous possibilities, but they seemed a bit tricky unless the class was perfectly behaved (visions of naughty kids depth-charging my good intentions). The 'trainer' told me, 'Yes, none of these strategies really works unless the kids are being pretty well behaved.' Which was lovely. And a fabulous way to lose £500 in a day. Still, lunch was good.

So sort out some training (especially if the school has committed part of its budget towards it; good Lord, free stuff!) and ask yourself, what do I want to learn or get better at? Take the school action plan into consideration by all means, but don't be limited by it – you will know, perhaps in conjunction with your line manager from what kind of training you would best benefit. You may, for example, have a burning ambition to learn sign language. As long as you can justify it in an educational context, go for it. If you *want* to learn it, chances are you might succeed and love it. But if you don't care for something, the trainer better be pretty … inspirational if they're going to light a fire in your heart.

---

[4] Anyone that claims they can teach you to inspire people should be marched out on a short plank at the end of a cutlass. Arr.

Plan another qualification (intelligence/wisdom)

I mean a real one this time, not a one-day jolly where you walk home with a certificate designed on Microsoft Publisher. I mean a home study course, or an MA, or anything that will benefit you as a person and as a teacher. If you're lucky the school may contribute towards some of the costs (I have known some excellent – and wealthy – standard bearer schools that have paid for entire courses). Even a PhD – why not? The knock-on effect for your self-esteem is enormous; your professional ability is enhanced by subject knowledge or skills, and you can bring that all back to the classroom, and incidentally to your CV. You may need to confer with loved ones and senior colleagues (perhaps they are the same person? I draw a veil) in case this affects the balance of your work and your life – will you need a day off school to complete it? A day every week? Tread softly. But if you don't ask ...

Plan a sabbatical (wisdom)

I don't just mean a rest, although by all means if you're feeling burned out it could be time for one (see later). But for some teachers a sabbatical is a possibility. This means taking (planned) time out of school[5] to pursue something that you consider to be either career- or life-enhancing. The educational upshot of this is that you return to the profession refreshed, intellectually and spiritually invigorated, and ready to bring your new life experiences into the classroom or simply into your professional space.

Of course the first question is finance; the school needs to cover your job, which they are often loth to do if it means training someone up or mentoring a rookie. But if you have someone else who can do it on the premises already, AND if you are pretty invaluable to the school, then you may have built up enough of an emotional bank account for the school to allow this. Again, their generosity will depend on the individual circumstance. Scholarships and bursaries are available for these kinds of enterprises, and the more entrepreneurial teacher will be able to discover sources of funding in other avenues – perhaps by cold-writing to companies and asking them if they would consider sponsoring you.

But to do what? The possibilities are limited only by your imagination; I took a sabbatical to do a School Teacher Fellowship at Corpus Christi, Cambridge University; I used the time to research and write a paper on the role of the teacher in history, and it was one

---

[5] Don't just stop showing up.

of the most rewarding experiences of my career as a teacher. Some people take time out to work in other sectors, or to shadow people, and a variety of companies have programmes to do just this: you will do your own research. Finally, you might even consider just jacking teaching in for a while and go and do this kind of thing – it's still a sabbatical, but you don't have the assurance of a guaranteed place anymore. But if you're brave and bold, this could be an option for you. One day you'll be too old to climb the pyramids on a camel, or something.

Participate in a disciplinary meeting (justice)

Some teachers avoid these kind of meetings as if they were toxic; they can certainly be intense, so perhaps the resistance is understandable. Many children fall foul of school rules, and for some of these, meetings will be necessary: re-integration meetings for pupils who need to reassure staff that past mistakes won't be made again; or reparation meetings between pupils; or meetings between pupils and their social workers, EAL advisors or whomever. These meetings are masterclasses in learning how to improve specific communication styles; if you're lucky, the person taking them understands the subtlety of communicating for different purposes; if you're not, they'll be arrogant, insensitive gasbags.

Whatever – try to get in on one of these meetings. There are an infinite number of excuses to justify your presence, such as 'taking minutes', but always respect the parameters and the decisions of the person conducting the meeting. Don't get involved, unless asked to by the chair, and otherwise keep your mouth shut. The point is to listen, and to hear how people talk successfully – or otherwise – to students. What would you have done that was better?

Visit an internal exclusion unit (justice/wisdom)

Many schools provide accommodation and educational provision for students who have had to be removed from mainstream schooling but have not been externally excluded (usually because externally excluding students has been made so damn hard that a child has to detonate a dirty bomb to be considered for a move). These, by whatever names they are known, are the internal exclusion units. They're like school purgatory. If yours is a foreign country to you, pop in. See if any of your students are there – perhaps you sent them down? It's a great opportunity to speak to often fractious students away from the situation they can't cope with in the first place, and you might be surprised by the different quality of relationships that exist in such environments.

Or, on the other hand, you might leave with your ass in your hat. But you'll never know unless you go.

Hold a door open (compassion)

You heard me. It's amazing how many adults operate in schools where civility appears to be checked in at the front gate. If we expect children to behave with manners, then it is imperative that we display those manners. I'm not advocating standing at the open door with a salute like a chimp, but the simple act of holding a door open until the next person comes through is a tiny but potent symbol of humanity and good will, that doesn't make you look like an idiot or an ingratiating toady. Of course make sure that someone is actually about to come through, or you'll look like a vegetable.

Plan an interesting piece of homework

Sometimes homework can be an afterthought, or a tag-on that meets some superficial school-based target. But done properly it can be an extension activity, and something that pupils actually want to do. With my year 7s I decided to get them to design and make a mandala – a Buddhist symbol of impermanence. I was amazed/delighted/stuffed to find how many kids baked cakes, built statues and carved intricate pieces of perishable materials. Now I just tend to mention that the best marks go to people who make cakes shaped like religious icons.[6]

Get to know the school data (practical wisdom)

Find out who in the school is responsible for the formal data on your children – it might be the SENCO, it might be a G&T coordinator, or it might be a data manager of some kind. It may even be (I hope) easily available on the system computer. Get information about your pupils' levels and achievements in other subjects, and contrast that with how they do for you, especially if the subjects bear some comparison – History and RS or English might be said to have some correlative value. This is a great way to nail down your understanding of who in your class has some kind of special need or statement of need and who is more able. It's always interesting when you find out that students massively over/under perform in your subject, and then you can ask why. These kinds of data also gives

---

[6] Of course I don't. I do talk them up a bit. Hard eating cakes shaped like Jesus, though.

you some clues (not conclusions, but clues) as to what you could do to emulate or avoid the practice of others…

Visit a local shop and ask them what they think of the students/school (compassion/wisdom)

Schools aren't enormous hermeneutically sealed bell-jars – they exist within larger, more diffuse communities. The children intersect with a million other Venn diagrams. How do they affect the people who work and live around the school? Find out – speak to shop keepers, vendors, street cleaners, anyone who comes into contact with them. Let them know that you're interested in what they have to say. In some cases, you'll hear what you don't want; in others, you might learn some secrets. But if they know that you're a face they can link to the school, not only have you done the school a bit of good PR, but you've started to build up contacts with the local community that really means something.

Learn about the school's history (wisdom)

There may only be a handful who know about the origins and history of the institution within which you work. That might not be a bad thing in some cases. Or, you might work in a mighty independent edifice, or an edifice of antiquity, where the names of the founders are tolled out in semaphore every Matins. But lay your hands on the written history of the building and the institution. Talk to people who have worked there since the days of Newton, perhaps the janitor, and find out the secrets of the batcave. Old buildings always have secrets.

Not only does this give you a practical knowledge of passages leading from the assembly hall to the dungeon, but it can give you ideas for activities and learning days that can engage the kids in a history that also belongs to them.

Start up a club (vigour/leadership)

Are you passionate about something? Do you moan that the kids never learn about 'x' anymore? Fine: start up an 'x' club after school. If you're enormously lucky there might be finance for it; if not, you may have to content yourself with a cupboard and your valuable time, with some photocopied posters. But it'll be *your* club; you can take it where you want. You can decide the curriculum and the aims. Freedom is bliss. Chess, Foreign Language film, go nuts.

Find something broken – and fix it (compassion/leadership)

Schools are large places. There are always things broken. Fix something. Of course, don't tackle anything structural or tread on the toes of the maintenance men. I simply mean find something in the school that physically could use some TLC. Is there an overgrown patch of grass? Organize a team of volunteers and get it chopped back. A graffiti wall? A batch of tables marbled with the chewing gum of yesteryear? Get some gloves and scrapers, and a strong stomach. It could be community work for earnest kids, or a form of sanction that doubles as a community intervention.

Sit an exam (courage/wisdom)
I'm not kidding. This is especially aimed at teachers of A-level, or senior children. Sit an exam at the same time as they do, either in class or externally. Have it independently marked by another teacher. Then brace yourself for the result. If it's good (and it should be), stand down. If it's not, then you, my friend, have identified a hole you could drive a school bus through. Fill it.

Start a revision class (responsibility/compassion/organization)
This is the kind of activity that can potentially gobble up your personal life, so read carefully. But it possibly wouldn't be too onerous to introduce a catch-up class once a month, say, and then sell, sell, sell it to the kids that need it the most. You might get a couple; you might get a flood. But you'll get kids who perhaps didn't understand at the time, or ones who just want to know more. Either way, can that be a bad thing? Of course, it's an easy way to stumble into enormous amounts of unpaid work, but you might be able to do a deal with your line manager. And also, it's enormously helpful.

Look back on your training year resources (wisdom/perspective/patience)
Don't they look sweet? Actually, you may even, after a few years of chalkface, knee deep in viscera, find that they look impossibly academic and intense. Either way, have a flick through the manuals and workbooks that guided you through the first wobbly eighteen months or so. If they look impossibly simplistic, then you can congratulate yourself on having absorbed and surpassed them. If they seem like a foreign language, then find out why; have you forgotten the lessons they tried to teach you, or are they simply wrong? Either way, you've learned something.

Get into school half an hour earlier (fortitude/organization)
If you're like me, this is like asking the tide to go away when it wants to come in. But, but, but. Persevere. Do you make it in seconds before

briefing or the bell? Congratulations – you operate with the lowest possible aspirations and expectations: how does it feel? Whatever time you get in, make a push for a week to get in half an hour earlier, and see how much extra you get done; see how much more relaxed you feel starting the day; see how many more resources you get ready. Half an hour at the start is worth an hour at the end.

I just made that up, but it's true.

Get your resources ready the day before/before the start of the week (vigour/wisdom)

This also depends on your current level of readiness. Many teachers persist in worrying themselves into an early grave by getting sheets photocopied, resources downloaded, PowerPoints planned etc. on the same day as execution. This is madness. All it takes is for one paper jam, one crash, one lost key, and you have just taken possession of the day from hell. Given the unavoidable observation that it takes exactly as long to do all this stuff the day before as it does on the day, then do yourself a favour – do it the day before, when it isn't vital, and you can handle banana skins without having a coronary.

Add some music to your day (perspective/calm)

You may not be a music person. You probably are. Music has a unique power to add theme and mood to your daily life. In the films, people always walk down the street to a theme tune, and miniaturization technology has allowed us all to emulate this. I'm not suggesting you strut into your class with headphones in and the *Theme from Shaft* defining your pimp walk (please, God, don't), but if you get a break, if you have half an hour to walk through the park at lunch time, treat yourself with your favourite music, or something that fills your heart with the good stuff. You'll still have it echoing around your head when you walk back into the class of mental year 9s. And it hath charms, I am told, to soothe the savage breast.

Spend a free period doing a corridor sweep (compassion/justice)

You know all that free time you get? Yeah, I know, I'm kidding, right? Take a compassion pill and help out your colleagues by doing at least one tour of duty every week – walk once, twice around the whole school and make sure everyone is where they need to be, and there are no 'lost' students pounding the beat. Check out the known bunking spots, the secret places. Yes, you might inherit a bit of hassle and follow-up, but you'll also be helping a load of your colleagues. Plus the naughty kids know you mean business.

Learn the names of five kids you don't know (wisdom/compassion)
Such a simple thing; but do this a few times and you'll start to get to know them all. We often compartmentalize our classes; the ones we teach and the ones we don't. Start treating the school community as one body, because that's how they probably see themselves.

Read a trade paper (wisdom)
This isn't just a gauche plug for the TES; there are scores of interesting educational blogs, online papers, and academic teaching journals that you can access (OK, maybe not all interesting). Pick one up and see what's going on in the great big world of education beyond the four walls of your institution. You, as Michael Jackson once said, are not alone.

Organize a blood drive (compassion)
You have blood, right? So, I assume, do the other teachers, unless they really are old school. Your older students might qualify (if they're 18) for this: call up the local blood team and ask them if they do mobile donation clinics. Or if they don't there's bound to be a local one that comes to town every now and then, like some chilling circus of vampires. It's a great sight, to see dozens of teachers staggering about looking tired (no change, really) and being extra careful with their forearms. And it's a terrific way to mobilize some community spirit in the school. See if there are any other charity gigs you can ally yourself with.

Decide you've had enough (courage)
Many teachers have a kid (sometimes many kids) with whom they have a kind of Groundhog Day experience, constant misbehaviour, on and on and on. Sometimes we get into the habit of letting it all slide, and accepting, 'That's just Connor.' And so it drags on.

Sometimes, it's time to draw a line and admit that we've become too tolerant of something that we once saw as intolerable. Look at the situation as if you were meeting the pupil for the first time; reboot the behaviour expectations. If they keep up with the same old attitudes and misbehaviours, then re-apply the sanctions that you might have tired of. Only this time, don't start to let it slide if things don't improve. This time, expect more than just an unpleasant status quo; get the senior staff involved, and ask them for a solution to the situation. It might be that the pupil gets taken to another class; it might be that the school is forced into a position where the child is offered alternative educational provision (read: excluded). But whatever happens, you will have made the classroom a safer and more educational place to be. Don't put up with bullies, especially if they're half your height and a quarter your age.

Decide *not* to take it home with you (perspective/wisdom)
If you're brand new at school, it often seems unavoidable to take books home in order to keep up with marking etc. And it may well be true. But there is a habit you should be trying to force yourself into – don't take it home with you if you can.

It is enormously important for your sanity and your stress levels that you keep school admin as much as possible within school boundaries. That means staying later and getting stuff done rather than humping it home with you and then humping it back in the next day. Not only does it give you a double-lug there and back, but it means that school work really starts to invade your private space. Home should be for *you*; school is for *them*. There is only so much of you to go around. The kids need you at your best. *You* need you at your best.

Remember: stay late rather than take it home. If you dash off on the dot of the bell, but you're taking work home with you, then you aren't really home; you're in a kind of swampy twilight world, a limbo where work isn't done properly because of distractions, and you never relax properly because of the work sitting there on the kitchen table, winking evilly at you. Slay the dragon at school. Save home for movies and curry.

Accept that there are some things you cannot change (wisdom/ fortitude)
Perhaps you've read this in a fortune cookie? It's still true. Look at all the things you have to do. Do you have enough time to do them all? Possibly not. So pick something that isn't vital and just accept that it won't get done. Watch carefully to see if the sky falls in. Be amazed when it does not. For example, your school might have a policy that stipulates that all books are marked on a weekly basis. But this week it's like the twelve tasks of Hercules to get it all done. In fact you're going to have to forgo bathroom visits and chewing your food if you're going to accomplish it all. Suddenly you are gripped by an amazing insight: if the year 8 books don't get marked this week … no one will die. I promise you. Let it happen, and don't feel guilty. Don't make a habit of it, but perspective is a wonderful thing. Get the really important things done, and sometimes you can afford to let the small fry slide by.

Reduce your marking demands (wisdom/organization)

Marking homework is a universal chore for teachers. But there are many ways to make it easier on yourself: you can set homework that can be peer marked by the children the next lesson (as long as it's factual or T/F); it can be revision; it can be something evaluated by a starter (learn the correct spellings of five key words) etc. Whatever you do, don't kill yourself with marking – less regular is better, if the marking and comments are good, rather than a manic timetable of scheduled marking that is light and superficial.

Rewrite your seating plan (courage/organization)

If you've got one – and I really hope you do – then it might be exactly the same one that you had from day one, particularly if you've had the same class in the same room for some time. Have a closer look at it; it this the way you really want them? Are there combinations that have sprung up as unlikely collaborations, designed to depth-charge your lesson? You can move them around whenever you want to. Do you want to? Take one class at a time.

Reboot your behaviour expectations (courage)

Repetition is the soul of security, and also the core of a behaviour management strategy. If the pupils know exactly where they stand with you, then they will learn to trust you in a way that is meaningful for an educator's relationship. They trust you to act in certain ways, and they know where they stand. If you don't have this kind of relationship, then the misbehavers will constantly be testing the boundaries with you, and your class will never be settled. So perhaps it's time for a reboot. This means, simply, reiterating your expectations of them, and what you believe/know they are capable of, both behaviourally and academically, with an emphasis on the optimistic. Tell them you believe they can succeed, but in order for this to happen, they'll have to do the following *gets out rules of classroom*….It can never be done often enough; you can reboot at any time in the year; if you teach anything but angels, you'll find that you occasionally have to reboot in the middle of a lesson ('Everyone stop what you're doing!')

Visit another school (wisdom)

Piece of cake. OK, this isn't an easy one to arrange, but when was anything valuable ever easy? Organize this as part of a greater school exchange program, or simply request it as continuing professional development. There is nothing quite like visiting another school for escaping the bubble that we all exist in within our own institutions. It becomes far too easy to see the customs and culture of our home turf as sacred cows, until it becomes barely imaginable that things could be any different. Seeing another school is like landing on another continent; the people look similar to your country of origin, but they look ... funny. Some of them are so extremely different, you feel like Charlton Heston.[7] So get out of your space shuttle and get down with your monkey brethren from another world. Every school is different. Not every school system can work in every school. But the comparison is valuable, even if it's just to learn how you *don't* want to do something...

What would Fonzie[8] do? (courage)

Confidence is one of the most important things to convey to the children; like little sharks, when they smell fear, they go for blood. But if you lack confidence, then have no fear; there is a substitute: *appearing* confident. Confidence isn't some magic quality someone possesses; it is in fact a trick. If you act confidently, people will treat you as if you are confident; you in turn *feel* confident. It's the original confidence trick. So if you want to come across with a sense of gravity and authority, you can simply act as though you were someone who had confidence.

How do you do that? One easy way is simply to imagine someone you respect and admire as a confident individual – and it doesn't have to be a real person either, or one you know; it can just be the visualization of that person. Consider, how would they stand? How would they speak? What would they say? Try to go with their flow, and see how it suits you. You might be surprised how easily this can take. Teaching, after all, requires you to adopt a persona of sorts, so act your way into better teaching.

Make a chart of your favourite students (wisdom/justice)

Be honest – do your personal feelings towards some students affect how you treat them in class? To some extent it's impossible to avoid this – good, pleasant, friendly and hard-working students tend to score highly on my reward scale. But it's interesting to note that this can go too far. So jot down your least favourite five, and your most favourite. Then ask yourself how often you punish or reward that

---

[7] You damn, dirty apes!

[8] Mythically lucky protagonist of popular 70s sitcom *Happy Days*. Lothario, miraculous mechanic and midget.

person. Is there a disparity? Consider the way that someone speaks to you, and ask yourself if it rubs you the wrong way because it they're not your type of person, or because it's rude, etc. This can really help you to see if you're as fair as you think. After all, no-one really thinks that they're unfair. But some people are. Funny that, isn't it?

Ask for help (courage)
Make today the day that you ask someone to help you. Some teachers exist in a crepuscular world of isolation, where they can see other teachers working around them, but they don't actually intersect with them. This is intolerable. You, me, everyone needs help sometimes, and you are either a god or a monster if you don't. So is there something you're struggling with? A child's behaviour? A strategy that isn't working? A part of the school structures that you don't quite get? Ask for help. Ask someone for advice. Ask someone. And listen – don't just nod and only take in what you agree with. If they disagree with you, ask why.

Go for a drink with colleagues (compassion/perspective)
Do I need to tell you this? But for some, when the school bell goes, they do too, and that kind of sunset segregation can be a shame. If you're new, one of the best ways to get into the school community is to go for a sharpener with the older hands. Be careful not to let it spiral into a session where you jettison your dignity, but a bit of R&R is an ideal way of integrating. Some of us get into the habit of never accepting invitations, and that's always your right. But sometimes it might be worth considering; have you cut yourself off too much? Maybe there are benefits to being less of a lonely island. Your disco needs you.

On the other side of this coin, if you've been there for a while, ask a newbie to the drinking hole, as long as it doesn't come across as an overture to tonsil hockey. It is often terrifying to be in a new school; make it a gentle landing. And don't let them get drunk.

Apply for a new job (courage)
This is similar to actually leaving, of course, but sometimes it doesn't hurt just to window-shop a little, even if you're happy where you are. You can either formally apply, or you can just go through the motions of doing so, right up to the moment of application (like Roman contraception). Unpack your CV out of the dungeon and dust it down, brush it off, and give it a coat of gloss and make-up. Drag it out into the modern era, make it a current document, not an

archive from history, like a time capsule. Check out the job ads, and ask yourself what you fancy. If nothing else, it'll make you feel like you're not left on the shelf.

Look at an old lesson and see if it's dead or alive (organization/ wisdom)

Have you been teaching the same lessons for a few years? In your first year you were an innovator, because you were probably starting from scratch. After that, perhaps you tinkered. Now you probably have a set of lessons you repeat every year. But are they good enough? Pick one lesson, perhaps a few weeks away and ask yourself, 'if I were designing this for the first time today, how would I construct a lesson to achieve the same aim?' I bet you would do it differently. I bet that you would do it better. So change it. One at a time, you don't have to kill yourself. In fact, please don't.

A different variant of this is to ask, how would I plan this lesson if I knew I was being observed? I don't mean formally observed by Ofsted (although it could be, although I have grave pedagogic reservations about assuming that their aims are your aims) but just if a colleague that you admire were dropping in to see how you teach; what would you do? Again, I bet it would be different. Is it different because you want to show off, or would it be different because it would actually be better? It's a good question. Answer it.

Don't take drugs

You should know this. But some teachers do, strangely enough. If you're one of them, then stop. And I also refer here to non-prescription, socially approved medications like alcohol. Would you like your children raised by a drunk? No, me neither. Anything stronger than a polo mint shouldn't go near your lips on a regular, unchecked basis, because children rely on you to look after them, physically and mentally. Some teachers forget the position they've agreed to take.

Look at the school action plan

Every school has a general plan of action for the coming year, and if you can't find one, then pull the ripcord and get the hell out. The school will have identified a number of priorities that it considers to be important and targets that it wants to achieve. I'm not suggesting that you should treat this document like the last tablet of Mormon, but it's interesting in ways other than the purely entertaining. What did you think the school priorities were? Did you think it had any? Do they differ from yours? Why/why not? Ask people who know why, and have a conversation about it. OK, I grant you, it's not a gripping exercise, but you'll be intrigued, I guarantee you, about why schools run the way they do, and the differences in opinion between foot soldiers and back-row pieces.

Know your data

I could have subtitled this: 'know your enemy', because data are easy to misinterpret, and there is a world of difference between data and conclusions; the former stand as they are, ungarnished, and the latter are creatures of value, opinion and perspective. Turning one into the other involves a process I can only describe as magic. Be very, very wary when someone in education tells you, 'The evidence shows that...' because I can almost certainly guarantee that nine times out of ten it bloody well doesn't, and it's being used as a smokescreen to authenticate a desired proposal.

Data mean a spectrum of things to people. For some it's the antithesis of education, reducing children to points on a graph, and crushing them with the predictive weight of statistics, reducing their free will to cruel destiny: this boy from that background will achieve this grade; his target is therefore that. The problem is that individuals can defy all the predictive powers of cold calculation. I once taught a boy who barely scraped through bottom set GCSE; at AS level he plunged into a U; I allowed him to continue through compassion more than design. And when the A2 exams with resits came in, he came away with a clean A. I resist the compulsion of data.

On the other hand, you need to know what your targets are – no teacher can escape the lure/snare of the fiscal model of education, and you need to know who is doing well, who isn't, and make some kind of estimate of which groups are underachieving. Why is this happening? What is the story behind the data? That's the thing. What do the figures mean to you? You will draw your own conclusions, and the search for meaning will be a revelation in itself.

Speak to someone at school – a data manager, an experienced teacher – who can talk you through the kind of data your school uses. See if you can push it further yourself. If you have a mind to it, or the experience, you can start to create your own models, spreadsheets and matrices. Data can be incredibly powerful, and most schools in the state sector have succumbed to adopting slavishly the principle of only valuing what can be measured. This is an international malaise, and perhaps a modern one, borne of a secular, empiricist world that can only appreciate what can be weighed.

Spend a day in a special unit

This could be an external exclusion unit or a dedicated school for EBD kids. But the only way to learn to deal with pupils with extreme spectrum behaviours is to be with them, and for some such kids, that means being up close with them, not keeping them at arm's length. You'll feel the fear of being with kids, many of whom quite frankly don't give a shit. How are you going to get through to them? Yet some of them can be reached. All your skills that you use in mainstream classrooms need to be sharp as a razor, and you'll find that the interpersonal side of your skill set gets tested to the maximum. Maintaining clear boundaries with children who think they can tell you to f*ck off as soon as they see you is a challenge you will never forget.

Shadow a senior member of staff

Note: this doesn't mean 'do anything they tell you to do' (I've seen it happen). If you want to know what command is like, spend a day with a member of the High Council, taking note of the variety of tasks they are called on to deal with throughout the day. If you thought that teaching offered a varied diet of experiences, wait until you assume some command, and have to deal with everyone from irate neighbours, to international appeals from partner schools in Zimbabwe.

Take on a student teacher

There is nothing – I say nothing – as good as generating clear indicators of how far you've progressed as taking someone less senior than you under your wing. No matter how often you look in a mirror, you'll never see your beard grow, and the same logic applies to your professional development; rare indeed are the times when you are conscious of the fact that you have improved or learned something. It normally takes external markers to show us that in fact we have changed at all. Taking on a trainee, apart from the fact that it's enormously beneficial to them and to the profession as a whole, is also the best way to re-examine your own standards and self-expectations. In the same way that becoming a parent can often transform a vagabond into a pillar of the community – I said 'can', not 'must' – so too can becoming a mentor/trainer be an exhilarating experience, as responsibility flushes your cheeks.

It also makes you realise a lot about what you've let slip. Do you know everything that they want to know, or have you been winging it in any way? Having a trainee will expose it. One great thing I try to remember is that while the trainee should be in no doubt as to your role and authority in the relationship, there should also be moments when you reflect on your own practice, and you can use the trainee for this purpose (legitimately, not scurrilously); ask them what they think of how you operate, and see if you can justify why and how you operate. The results are often revealing.

Finally, you have the satisfaction of knowing that you have contributed to the creation of another teacher. In that respect you're a bit like Baron von Frankenstein.

Here are some more exercises aimed at matching your ambitions to your abilities:

Learning walks

A common tool from middle-management upwards: as the name suggests, take a tour of the school in which you work. Look at what's really going on in the rooms, in the corridors, the public areas. How would it look if you were a complete stranger to the school? Or even teaching. This is a wonderful, rewarding, refreshing way to pull back and see the school as a whole, not a bundle of successive rooms. You can have a specific focus (behaviour, how many cover teachers, pupils parked outside classes, etc.) or just let it wash over you like the Buddha. Start to see the institution as an organism, not a cellblock, and see how one organ affects another....

Work scrutiny

If you've led any kind of team in a school, this will have been part of your experience. Gather in a selection of colleagues' school books and evaluate them for any number of criteria. See how much work different teachers get out of the same class, or assess literacy, formative commentary, etc. All such scrutiny has to be analyzed with a keen eye for context – a teacher's class might show little written work, but be working in other ways. Of course, you don't have to be a leader of men to do this: why not simply ask to see other colleagues' books at a department meeting. Resist the temptation to laugh, or burst with horror.

Get a bloody haircut

You heard me. It's a disgrace. There are few physical garnishes or cosmetic tweaks that have such a profound modifying effect on one's self-image as a hair cut (I believe that women refer to it as 'having their hair done'. I have no idea what goes on, but I gather it involves tea, conversation, and a zero added on to the bill). People look at you differently. You look at you differently. People ask you, charmingly, 'Have you had a haircut?' and you can look at them like they're stupid. It's a good, simple psychic reboot, particularly to punctuate a new term/year.

Suit up

Adding stilts to the haircut, go for a new school wardrobe. The effect of smart attire on the way you are perceived is enormous in school. Look around you, at the teachers by your side. Do they come into work with tailored two-pieces and polished shoes? Do they look organized and efficient? The answer is yes. They do. Or have they failed to iron their shirts, or scorned footwear in favour of airing their calloused hobbit feet in sandals? Do they look like an art teacher? The answer is also yes. In an ideal world, it wouldn't matter what we wore; we would all be judged by our inner beauty or something. We are still waiting for this world.

Until it arrives, people will judge you by your appearance – isn't it awful? Children are fearsomely prone to stereotype, which is another unpleasant fact, but there you go. You're welcome to try to change the world from your wardrobe, but don't hold your breath while you do so. You can surf the wave of their expectation, or swim against it. Good luck with that.

But this isn't merely an exercise in appeasement; it's also a powerful symbol to yourself: today I mean business; today I'm here as a professional, not a dilettante. If you're already pretty smart, tighten up a notch and see how it feels. I personally like to Get Smart until I get to the point where I start to feel slightly uncomfortable; then I know I'm smart enough. You will find your own point or equilibrium.

Lay off the smokes if you can

I pay tribute here to Christopher Hitchens, the raconteur and reluctant smoker penitent. While teaching isn't in the same league as lumberjacking, it's still a job that requires physical effort, long periods on your feet, and plenty of walking around. You need to be in reasonable shape in order to do a good job. Of course, a six-pack and gym buns will do little to assist your teaching other than draw admiring glances from the janitor, so, like vitamin A, there comes an optimal point beyond which further conditioning fails to assist. Aristotle and Plato both made similar points, encapsulated by the famous 'Healthy mind in a healthy body' aphorism, not because bench-pressing will assist your practice, but because in order for the mind and character to perform unimpeded by infirmity and torpor, the body needs to be able to work at a certain level of efficiency. A surfeit is useless, but a deficiency is a deal-breaker.

Incidentally, although in this book I've focused on virtues of character, Aristotle also had a list of physical virtues that could be worked on (in perhaps a more obvious way than character – we're far more familiar with the concept of working our biceps than our optimism). These virtues included strength, dexterity, agility and, less obviously, 'a deep voice'. I wasn't going to mention it, in case it made Aristotle look stupid, but I think he's safe.

Look after your body. It is often something that many teachers pay little attention to or, as most of us do, only when it starts to make grumbling noises that we can no longer ignore. I am a fairly average man; my weight and shape fluctuate beautifully throughout the year, from trim Titan to cuddly eccentric. I have enjoyed periods in my life where I have actively felt the sensation of being fit; of feeling that my body could do everything I wanted, and have some left over. I heartily recommend it. If you want to feel great about yourself, and carry that energy into the classroom, then get some trainers on. And then run a bit.

15 Keeping in Shape – Perpetual Professional Development and Following the Right Career Path

'LISTEN I GET IT YOU'RE TOP DOG IN THIS PLACE NOW - WHO DO YOU NEED ME TO TAKE OUT?'

But what about furthering your career as a teacher in new and interesting ways? There are many ways to be a teacher and still do something else in school. There are a vast number of opportunities in the labyrinth of the school: upwards into senior management, where you'll be carried along in a sedan while you breathe bottled air from the Himalayas and eat peeled grapes. Or sideways into undiscovered countries of function and utility. And sometimes you achieve escape velocity and leave school entirely. What are the things you can do to become not just a better teacher, but a different kind of teacher?

There are several different ways to improve in this manner:

1. learn more about your subject
2. learn more about management
3. learn more about a different area of education: SEN, EAL, pastoral, curricular
4. learn about something entirely different.

I'm of a generation that saw *Friends* the first time round, which in the nineties was seen as zeitgeisty and achingly hip; now it looks as contemporary as a typewriter. One of the characters, Rachel, was a ditzy, needy relationship car-crash. At one birthday party she broke down in tears when she realised she was thirty: as a child she had decided that she wanted to be a mother by the time she was 35. But that would mean she would have to get pregnant at 34; and that would have to take place at least a year after she got married. And of course, she didn't want to get married until she'd courted with some guy for at least a year or so. By which calculation she realised that she would have to meet her life partner .... that day. Cue: more floods.

The Holistic Approach to the meaning of life

Rachel's somewhat Machiavellian calculus aside, it is extraordinary how easy it is for us to lose sight of what our overarching goals are in life. It is similarly simple to forget that we even have such things. Many of us exist on a daily basis, simply getting by from one day to the next. Now if you're a fan of considering the lilies, or Buddhism generally, you might not see that as problematic. But while it might be a reasonable recipe for daily contentment, it lacks one crucial ingredient. Your life isn't just a collection of individual days, nor is it a seventy-year snapshot: it's both. When we seek meaning and value in our lives, we do many things:

1. We consider our histories retrospectively, chronologically.
2. We invent narratives within that timeline, picking out those things that strike us as important. This is a combination of the active and the passive. Active, because we deliberately construct stories that suit our own tastes; passive, because we construct these narratives out of tastes and values that already exist within ourselves.
3. We also project into the future; we extrapolate our probable crypto-futures, and attach our ambitions or avoidance on to them accordingly. In other words, we to some extent aim for the futures we imagine.
4. We consider what matters to us right now, as well as what matters to us generally. The identification of these definitive points is a part of what we mean by the phrase 'us'. Who am I? To some extent, I am a collection of the things that matter to me.

So what matters to you? It's important to decide (and discover: it's partly passive) this. We take stock of all the things we have experienced, and we categorize, evaluate and assess their meaning to us. Then we imagine how we might attend more to those values, and aim, as it were, for them in the future, based on our own evaluations.

Example: I used to be a fan of comic books and Arthurian literature;[1] I read them for years – looking back, I can see how concepts like altruism, chivalry and sacrifice affected me. So in order to put these values into practice I introduce opportunities into my life where these values can be replicated in a meaningful way. Perhaps I throw my cloak on a puddle for a lady, or take a bullet for the President. Or maybe I just become a teacher and promise myself to show manners to everyone, whether they deserve them or not ...

What matters to you? You are the final arbiter of that conversation, as you are the last word and the only witness to the internal monologue of your mind. But you might be surprised by the opinions of others. Speak to people who really, really know you, who are articulate enough to express it in an efficient way. I've been told a few home truths about what I'm really like by people who knew me too well. Sometimes it's not pleasant, but by God it can be sobering.

---

[1] As you can imagine, I was swatting off girlfriends with a spanner.

Where do you see yourself in five years time?

If you've ever had that conversation at a staff appraisal, you'll know that it's a tricky one to answer.[2] But seriously: where do you see yourself? It's a good question. Although I strenuously attempt to avoid sounding like an NLP textbook, anyone who doesn't have a plan about where they're going will end up where life takes them, rather than where they want to go. Amazingly, many people have no mid-term plans, only short-term ones that are constantly met, missed or reset depending on the prevailing weather of life. But big plans are important. If you have a big plan in your life, you at least have a chance of reaching it. Without a goal, an aim, you live through a collection of individual days, and miss out the opportunity for your life to have larger arcs and narratives of larger meaning.

Of course you can't plan for life. But you can plan. That will take you immeasurably closer to where you want to be. Like our narcissistic fictional friend[3] Rachel, have a long-term target with big bold brushstrokes of ambition. By all means make them aspirational, for God's sake, *please* make them aspirational. 'A man's reach should exceed his grasp,' quoth Robert Browning, 'Or what's a heaven for?' Quite. Reach for the Pole Star, as long as your ambitions are achievable by human effort and initiative. 'Winning the lottery' isn't a particularly credible ambition – that's a daydream, a pleasant diversion (some would say distraction) from genuine ambition: own a company; run a school; be married with children; open an orphanage. I don't know, whatever you want. Then plan backwards from that point, and ask what you need to have done in order to achieve it, step by step, backwards in time, until you reach your present point. It's simple to do. So why don't we?

Life gets in the way. We live in a bubble of our own concerns, like shire horses, blinkered against anything that distracts or scares us off our immediate path. When I cycle through the traffic of London, my focus of attention is very, very narrow: normally I'm aware of the ten or so metres in front of me, and the metre immediately to the left and right of me. That's a corridor of focus, and all else is driven out by expediency, survival and utilitarian considerations. Once in a while, I'll look up to see the greater picture ahead, but it's mostly autopilot and tunnel vision. When do I decide the route of my journey? Before

---

[2] Although my personal favourite answer I ever heard was, 'Standing on a pile of maimed bodies holding an axe as my armies conquer Persia.'
[3] The best kind.

I leave; *not* when I'm dodging JCBs and enthusiastic, polite lorry drivers.

When do you plan your journey? Not when you're in the middle of a lesson. Not when you're dodging spit, or taking a child to the nurse, or writing up an incident report. And sometimes that means never.

Why did you become a teacher? Was it because you lacked the ambition to do anything else? Did you fall into it, deterred from other avenues by a paralysis of imagination? Probably not. It probably appealed to you; something in the career resonated with you like a tuning fork or a crystal glass. At some point it sang your song. Does it still do that? Where do you see yourself in five years time? Take the time to think about it.

Which leads me to my first exercise any teacher should do from time to time, perhaps once a year:

Take a trip somewhere school is a distant memory

I don't need to tell you to take holidays. But some holidays recharge, whereas others deplete. It is all very well to book yourself a week caning the bars of Ibiza and Magaluf for seven days in a row and getting back the night before INSET, but your body will hate you. I will hate you.[4] Because you will re-enter the teaching treadmill at the same speed you left it, and you will sink further into the role without the perspective you need. Once in a while, take a holiday that will genuinely reboot. My preference is for the Highlands of Scotland, particularly the Orkneys, where life is slower, the scenery is severe and awesome, and you have as many cliffs, waves, hills and warm, dry pubs you could ever need to accommodate. It could be anywhere – the Gobi Desert or Somerset – but find yourself somewhere you can completely remove yourself from teaching, see things that you never normally see, and get in touch with the you that isn't a teacher. For God's sake, have a few long lies-in; get some early nights; see an old friend.

Just do whatever it takes to get away from the exercise wheel of anxiety and immediate, urgent tasks of which teaching is comprised. Stare at some stars with a glass of wine in your hand and consider what you want to do with the rest of your life. I can't avoid sounding slightly spiritual when I say that every day you have is a gift; your life is ripe with opportunities and possibilities; you yourself are some kind of miracle. What can't you do? Believe this, even just a little bit, because it's true. What matters to you? What, on your deathbed

---

4   I'm kidding. I love you.

would you like to remember having done? Famously, no one on their death beds ever says, 'I wish I'd spent more time in the office.' What do you want to have as a legacy? What could you be proud of?

Do this at least once a year. I call it 'an appointment with your own soul', whether you believe in such a thing or not. This is very much part of the process that Aristotle also describes. Because one of the problems with a Virtue Ethics approach to your life is that there will often be times when virtues will conflict, and you are left with the responsibility to decide which one should predominate.

Example: Your sister has committed a crime, and the police ask you if you have any information about it. Do you submit to familial loyalty or civic duty? Which one wins?

Virtue Ethics resists the attempt to provide an easy, legalistic answer; in fact it rejects that approach entirely. As an alternative it suggests that we need to try to understand the bigger picture of our lives, and generate an understanding of the holistic entirety of who we are, and what kind of lives we want to live. Once we have settled on a clearer idea of this – consider it a map – then we can make the smaller decisions, based on whether those actions correspond or defy the bigger picture. Which means that at some points and contexts we will act one way; at another, another. That is part of the complexity and the subtlety of the system. It relies on you being an adult, and taking responsibility for your own life.

By now you should realize one simple truth about becoming a better teacher:

Teacher training goes on forever.

Like concrete in the churn, the minute you stop moving, you start to solidify. Do you want to be set concrete in a mixer? No. The matter is settled. Of course, this isn't some kind of attack on the formal training process of teaching;[5] the year/s you spend learning to be a teacher are pivotal. But you must, must, must propel and drive your own teacher training throughout your career. As Sue Bubb says in *Helping Staff Develop in Schools*:

'The process is what's important: development is something that is within the person all the time, not something done or provided for them.'

---

[5] Unlike some of the more fashionable educational experts, I think that the formal schooling process does have a special importance; it is moronic to say that everyone is a life-long learner. Of course, in some senses, it's impossible to stop learning throughout your life, no matter what you do. But, y'know, some people don't learn very much, that's all I'm saying ...

This is especially true of teacher training, post-college. How many INSETS have you sat through where senior staff attempted to crowbar some scheme or initiative into your coupon? Many, many times, I suspect. You can't really learn unless there is some motivating factor. For students, we rely on an element of coercion, an element of relationship-building and an element of interest. For adults the process is similar, but more complicated. We cannot really be forced, not in a meaningful way. It is important to take ownership over our own futures by taking ownership over our own progression. Who's the most important participant in this process? YOU are.

In school training

In many ways, schools are the perfect place to improve your teaching skills, not some laboratory environment removed from the classroom experience (educational researchers, please take note). But if we're not careful, the common teacher experience of training can be pretty lousy. If I asked you to raise your hands if you've ever sat through an interminable three hours of bum-numbing horror as you poured your heart out onto a piece of sugar paper as some ghoul with a PowerPoint sucked the last wisps of your soul out through your nostrils like some vampiric facilitator, then I imagine I'd be facing a sea of hands right now. It is perhaps understandable that schools wish to deliver and share best practice, but in my experience we often do this badly.

I present you with this oddity: schools are meant to be institutions specializing in the education of others; yet when it comes to training teachers en masse, they often prove themselves to be completely inadequate. We fret and worry about breaking up activities to sustain interest in the classroom; we provide starters and plenaries, and avoid PowerPoints swamped with data, etc. But when it comes to teacher training, suddenly these rules get jettisoned in favour of presentations that range from interminably statistical and data-driven, to moronic and infantile. Odd, isn't it?[6]

---

[6] You cannot help the quality of your in-school development days, unless you either choose to participate in the presentation itself, participate in an energetic and focused way, or hijack it like a cultural terrorist. I've seen wel-planned, dreary sessions torpedoed by damn-your-eyes mavericks who stopped giving a monkeys *years* previously. 'This is sh*t,' they say loudly right at the start, and then repeatedly throughout. Funny, but rather awkward.

Do not be ashamed of wondering if the quality of development you receive is sufficiently challenging – it's your development that's at stake. I'm not suggesting you sit at the back and shout *bollocks* a lot, but all teachers have to become critical friends to their own education. If you're not learning from a training session, and you're genuinely trying, then you are perfectly entitled to feel a sense of being cheated. Schools usually put a lot of effort into training, but with very varied results. It's entirely possible that you're being short-changed.

More exercises to help you decide the direction of your career

Make a list of your interests and hobbies

This sounds like the least interesting but easiest part of writing your CV. But the point here is to try to make a genuine list of the things you *really* like to do, the things you do when you have free time. It could be a formal hobby like playing football, prospecting for gold or whatever, or it could be abstract, like meeting people, or making people laugh. What do you like? Then ask yourself how these activities and interests could be carried over into your teaching career. If you have a formal skill/interest (like playing chess, or gardening) then think about ways in which you introduce these into your professional sphere. As Mary Poppins once said, once you find the fun in the work *snap!* the work's a game.[7]

There is a formal process for advancing your career, and an informal one. The formal process involves climbing the ladder of the school; the informal one means developing yourself sideways, into roles that suit your style, your temperament and your skill set. At the same time, this opportunity allows you to develop your skills in ways that might never have occurred to you. You may have had a career prior to teaching. What aspects of that previous life can you bring to the table? I used to run nightclubs, and at first sight the ability to quell drunks, mix drinks, and duck punches from transvestites doesn't seem to transfer easily. But I have found that it came in enormously handy in helping students apply for jobs and write CVs and covering letters, as I had processed thousands in my career. See what you can bring. What are you good at?

That last question is vital, and I'll add two others:

---

[7] Mary Poppins was a home tutor who didn't have to contend with a National Curriculum. Or physics.

1. What are you good at?
2. What do you enjoy?

If you were to draw up a list answering both, I would be unsurprised if there was an enormous amount of overlap; we are often good at what we enjoy, and enjoy what we're good at. On one level this is intuitively obvious: when we enjoy something, we practise it more, and usually become better at it. When we become better at something, we usually enjoy it more. The two are locked into a cycle so neatly it's a wonder we don't all become prodigies and geniuses, given that one engenders another. Oh yes: laziness, I forgot, that's another factor.

Atlas Shrugged: the role of willpower in changing your world

If this sounds a little Ayn Rand,[8] it's not meant to be. In teaching your achievements are often the product of your will, your desire to change things, and your desire to master your own weaknesses – the sum total of your virtues working together in harmony. But this argument is open to endless claims of ideology – that such a position is essentially the libertarian/right-wing position that we are responsible for our own destinies, and that any accolades or condemnation we acquire is entirely earned. This would be laudable, were it not for the fact that it becomes another way of describing karma, the idea that there is a universal arbiter between this life and the next, and that we all get what we deserve. How comforting. How untrue.

The left-wing response is that we are products of social processes that are often/usually beyond our direct control; being born into a low station is an enormous barrier to social mobility; the children of the fortunate have a head start; a starving man in Somalia cannot simply get on his bike and look for work. This argument seems equally convincing, and seems to lead to the death of the idea that willpower is the rocket fuel of ambition and success. Which one is correct?

Such dichotomies are false, as most dualistic systems are: in the debate between free will and determinism, for example, an easy compromise is to admit that in some matters we are free and in

---

[8] Twentieth-century philosopher, famous for expressing the view that kindness was a weakness, and compassion a defeatist motivation. A real sweetheart.

others we may not be; and in this case, the solution is simple: you are the product of forces beyond your control AND forces within your control; you make the most of/endure the former, while developing the latter.

It simply isn't good enough to blame the child of an alcoholic prostitute for his own awful predicament; all the statistics will have such a boy chained to the mast of drug abuse and poverty. He may well have the same level of willpower as the child of privilege, but the challenges they face are unequal, and while the latter may possess the character to succeed in his personal circumstances, the former falls at the first enormous hurdle.[9]

Example: Two children of equal determination and integrity. Child one comes home every day to a father that beats him, and tells him school is pointless. Child two comes home to a supportive nuclear unit. Which one faces the bigger challenge to try hard at school? Which one is more likely to fall?

Willpower, optimism and hope are the catalysts and the fuel that propel us through the sky and into space; but some of us face obstacles that require us to burn more fuel. The tension between the two circumstances – willpower and context – is crucial in determining how successful we are. A wise man will attempt to put himself in circumstances where temptation is reduced, where obstacles are fewer. A woman in a dysfunctional relationship can leave the relationship and alter the ground rules of her life; or she can stay and try to fix matters, exhausting her reserves and her will on a daily basis, until there is nothing left for her own ambition. Willpower and determination are depletable resources; if we waste them on one activity, we reduce them for others. They can be restocked, and we can do so through activities that assist the process (relaxing, spending time with those who love us, doing things we enjoy), but even though they are abstract, they have a tangible and finite graph.

What does this mean in teaching?

There will only be so much that you, as one person, can do. I've already discussed the need to accept your limitations and be realistic about what is possible, not to curb your ambition but to focus it.

---

[9] I'm not so crass as to imagine that wealth immunizes you from privation or distress, but it sure helps to pay a lot of bills.

Your ambitions can still be aspirational and sky-high, but they must be chained to reality, just as a doctor who refused to accept death in his care would resign in misery after a month. But stay alive to the possibility that there is an enormous amount of impact you can have: both personally, to individual children, to your classes, and to the school in general. If the situation you face is untenable, how can you change the situation? If you face a problem, ask yourself if this is something YOU can fix, or someone else can help you to fix. After that, ask yourself if you can fix the situation that creates the problem. If the answer is still no, then endure; or take even more radical action, including removing yourself from the situation entirely (see: changing schools).

And consider this too for the people you work with: you may think them lazy, or unambitious; but do you know that? Do you know your colleagues' ambitions or the difficulties they face? Understanding their context can hold the clue to working with them, and helping them to work. So too should you consider this in relation to your students; while it is useful to have absolute standards by which all students must abide, there also needs to be a place for wisdom and temperance in your practice, to allow for circumstance. If a child lives in a swamp of hatred and mistrust, it's not going to be enough to tell him to be polite. Maybe it should be, but it just isn't. Deal with it. Consider ways to support the child, at the same time as having high expectations that push him out of his comfort zone.

The quest for the work/ life balance

This is a mythical beast – there is no point of balance, in the same way that there is no one posture to adopt that will carry you across a high-wire; you shift and hustle and keep yourself upright as you walk along and as the winds blow. Just as there is no set level of virtue required for every circumstance, so too does your work/ life ratio depend on the context. There will be times that taking work home might very well be the best thing to do – your first year of teaching, the night before an Ofsted, for example, before a big interview – and times that you'd be mad even to think of carrying it home. Some nights you'll stay up and mark until the birds come out, and sometimes you'll leave on the dot, walking straight into a pair of heels and a nightclub.

How do you find this balance? This is especially hard, because often we're too close to ourselves to notice when the balance is being tipped. It can take a close friend or colleague to pull the alarm cord for you when you're turning into a job slave, or when you're steering off the straight. Because, to be sure, teaching is an enormous duty and responsibility, and sometimes you will have to forgo personal pleasures in order to meet the demands of the role. And although there's a large 9-5 element to it, there are considerable stresses to be taken home, as well as work of a practical nature. Sometimes your life will have to take predominance, otherwise you'll go mad; sometimes it will have to take a back seat. And of course both sides are your life; don't mistake one as being YOU, and the other .... well, the teaching you. They're both you, mysteriously.

There is one aspect of your home life that you need to get right – your sleep pattern. This is no career for the cavalier night owl. The kids need you fresh – fresher than them at least – and emotionally and intellectually sharp, to deal with all those crises of virtue we've been discussing. If you drag your sorry ass into school looking like Keith Richard's toaster, then expect no mercy, because the kids certainly won't give you any. I used to tumble into bed after the dawn chorus, and rise again with the setting sun. Perhaps you did too? You can stop doing this now. You have a duty to others. Incidentally, if you have small children then you deserve a bloody medal, because I'm not sure how you do the middle-of-the-night thing and still rock up on time. Do you take drugs?

Many opportunities for development in the school can be classed as either being pastoral – student general welfare, behaviour, relationship with the home – and curricular – what do they learn, how is it taught, etc. You may already have a strong affinity with either. Ask yourself what you're more passionate about – uniform standards, or the best way to differentiate in a classroom? Good teachers are interested in the whole thing to some extent, but you'll find an intuitive attraction to one end of the spectrum. If your interests are pastoral, then you'll be suited to roles and areas such as Head of Year/Learning, mentoring, attendance and punctuality; if you fancy an academic path, then look to heading departments then faculties. Either role will take you into senior management, as they are broadly concerned with both.

Do you really want to be a senior manager/ leader?

This is a very good question. There is an unquestioned assumption that the ambitious teacher will eventually end up in senior roles at school, and of course in many cases this is absolutely the right career path. After all, if you're passionate about education and making a difference to children; if you've ever felt frustrated because your school doesn't do the things the way you would if YOU were in charge, then this is the perfect solution – step into the shoes of power and make the changes. Your problems have been solved, right?

Maybe not. As you progress up the leadership spine, two things happen simultaneously: you get paid more (which is fabulous, if extrinsic to your professional role), and you teach less. This is inevitable. Your teaching timetable dwindles to allow you to engage with all the different duties required of you (many of which, it seems to me, involve filling in online forms and monitoring lunch queues). So you spend less and less time in the classroom, and more and more time managing.

Is that what you want from your teaching career? To become so successful that you eventually no longer teach? It is the eternal contradiction inherent in any promotion; when I worked in restaurants we used to promote incredible, experienced bartenders into the management team until we had traded an expert in one field for an amateur in another. Of course, it's a natural way to progress, but it's a huge loss to the first profession. If you are a teacher, and you're passionate about teaching, you should feel no shame at all about the desire or ambition to remain, primarily, a teacher. Schools need people like you; children need people like you; the experience you accumulate is exactly what is needed to turn children's education and lives around. This entire book is dedicated to the development of you as a teacher and the profession as a whole. Its aim is to make you consider that teaching IS a profession, and needs as many professionals as possible. Experience is a vital component of that.

Of course, there is always the risk that you will go stark, staring insane if you stay too long. The teacher who stays for more than a few years will notice one of the awful, unspoken enemies of education: entropy. Eventually every teacher notices one truism: 'hey, I'm teaching the same lessons I did last year.' This is something non-teachers like to ask us at parties; isn't it boring? The answer is, yes, it is. Do that for long enough, put up with enough grief from enough kids, and watch the teacher dissolve in an existential puddle of cynicism and nihilism.

How to combat this? Keep moving, keep moving, keep the concrete from setting. Do the exercises I've described in this book, plus any you can think of yourself. The key is to try something new, constantly to challenge yourself, and recognize when something is worth retaining as the wisdom of the ancients, and when dogma needs to be challenged. And bear in mind that a lot of the dogma you encounter will come from yourself. Take on extra responsibilities, and master them. Then, when you tire of them, take on other responsibilities, and drop the original ones, because you can't do everything successfully. Let someone else learn how to do your job; perhaps you can mentor them as you leave the position.

Eventually there are many opportunities for teachers who need more challenge: in England and Wales there is the option to become an Advanced Skills Teacher (AST), where the teacher spends the equivalent of one day a week sharing their skills and experience with other schools, which to me sounds the very ideal way of improving teaching practice in different clusters of schools. Other options include going into teacher training, becoming a Head of Learning/ Year; Faculty Head; SENCO; Gifted and Talented Coordinator; literacy coordinator, and a whole host of other twists on teaching. You can mentor kids with other agencies, either private or state-funded; you can become a home tutor; you can do supply, if you have a high tolerance for bullshit and misery. You can consult for commercial agencies, such as television companies; you can lecture; you can run external INSETS. You can teach abroad; or in a private school, if you're state-trained (or vice versa if you don't mind kids who can't recite the *Iliad* yet). You could even move into writing educational books for teachers....

Conclusion

Whatever you choose to do, keep learning and keep caring. This is a profession with an enormous potential to drain you of every erg of humanity and happiness – anything that involves dealing with the public on a large scale has the potential to do this. People are just so ... well, they're so bloody awkward. Even if only a small percentage of the people you teach are assholes, that still means that there's an asshole along every minute. The longer you stay the more assholes you meet. It's inevitable. Every week, they can chip-chip-chip away at you. It's no wonder that one in five teachers leaves in the UK within five years. Think of that – all that experience and time, wasted, just lost to the world, like tears in the rain. The average life expectancy of male teachers after retirement is ... wait for it....five years. Yeah, they don't big that up in the recruitment campaigns. I bet deep-sea miners have a higher survival rate.[1]

And yet ..... this is one of the most vital professions in the world. It is ancient. I've heard that either the assassin or the prostitute is humanity's oldest trade but that doesn't scan for me at all. Surely one of the oldest professions must be the teacher; the man or woman whose job is to pass on the knowledge of the tribe, the clan, the community? Once they taught their first cave-kids, *then* came the assassins and the hookers.[2]

If I haven't made it clear how important I think this role is to your community, to the entire world, then I've wasted 70,000 words or so.[3] I am desperately proud to be a teacher, and not for some fuzzy reason like I want to bring joy and happiness to the lives of children – I'm not Barbara Streisand[4] – but because it matters; the job matters, and

---

[1] *And* their canaries.

[2] Bottom set, probably.

[3] You may still feel this to be the case. I can only hope you paid for the book already. Sucker.

[4] To my knowledge.

you will matter the better you perform your role. You play a small but vital part in the formation of another person; you assist their progress into society; you aid and abet their flourishing. Can there be anything finer? Play it right, and this job can lift you up every single day. It can fill you with achievement and pride. I wake up every day and look forward to my job – and that's no idle boast. If you're suited to teaching, then you should want to be the best teacher you can be. Not just because it's the right thing to do (it is) but because by doing so you will find yourself flourishing in ways you couldn't have imagined.

Plato and Aristotle taught us this. Virtue Ethics defines happiness as being good; and they defined being good as performing your role to the best of your ability. Being moral is therefore intrinsic to being good at your job, which is in turn intrinsic to your satisfaction in life.

Now isn't that a goal worth pursuing?

Good luck, and spread the love.

References and Further Reading

Aristotle (2005), *The Art of Rhetoric*, trans. Hugh Lawson-Tancred (London: Penguin Classics Ltd)

—(2004), *The Nichomachean Ethics*, trans. J. A. K. Thomson; rev. Hugh Tredennick; introduction Jonathan Barnes (London: Penguin Classics Ltd)

—(1996), *Politics*, trans. T. A. Sinclair (London: Penguin Classics Ltd)

Benn, Melissa (2011), *School Wars: the Battle for Britain's Education* (London: Verso Books)

Darwall, Stephen ed. (2003), *Virtue Ethics* (Oxford: Blackwell Publishing)

Feynman, Richard P. (2001), *The Pleasure of Finding Things out: The Best Short Works of Richard P. Feynmen*, ed. Jeffery Robins (London: Penguin Books Ltd.)

Furedi, Frank (2003), *Therapy Culture: Cultivating Vulnerability in an Uncertain Age* (Abingdon: Routledge)

—(2009), *Wasted: Why Education isn't Educating* (London: Continuum International Publishing Company)

—(2006), *Where have all the Intellectuals Gone? Confronting 21st century Philistinism* (London: Continuum International Publishing Company)

Goldacre, Ben (2008), *Bad Science* (London: HarperCollins)

Hill-Jackson, Valerie and Chance W. Lewis (2010), *Transforming Teacher Education: What Went Wrong with Teacher Education, and How We can Fix it* (Sterling VA: Stylus Publishing)

Hume, David and Peter Millican (2008), *An Enquiry Concerning Human Understanding.* (Oxford: Oxford University Press)

Jones, Ken (2003), *Education in Britain: 1944 to the Present.* (Cambridge/ Oxford: Cambridge Polity Press in association with Blackwell Publishing Ltd)

Kant, Immanuel, ed. Mary Gregor (1997), *Groundwork of the Metaphysics of Morals.* (Cambridge: Cambridge University Press)

Lawton, Denis and Peter Gordon (2002), *A History of Western Education Ideas.* (London: Woburn Press)

Lee, Harper (1966), *To Kill a Mockingbird* (Harlow: Heinemann)

MacIntyre, Alasdair (1997), *After Virtue: a study in moral theory.* (London: Gerald Duckworth & Co.)

Marrou, Henri I. (1964), *History of Education in Antiquity.* (New York: Penguin USA, New American Library)

McCulloch, Gary ed. (2005), *The RoutledgeFalmer Reader in History of Education.* (Abingdon: Routledge)

Moore, Alan and Dave Gibbons (1987), *Watchmen* (London: Titan Books)

Simon, Brian (1994), *The State and Educational Change: Essays in the History of Education and Pedagogy.* (London: Lawrence & Wishart)

Thelin, John R. (2004), *A History of American Higher Education.* (Baltimore and London: The Johns Hopkins University Press)

White, T. H. (1996), *The Once and Future King* (London: HarperCollins/ Voyager)

Index

academies 35, 39
Adonis, Lord 37
aims of education 9, 19
American education 45
anthropic principle 97
Appleby, Sir Humphrey 95
apprenticeships 28
Aristotle 22, 44, 58, 71, 79, 81, 96, 137, 142, 184, 190, 200
assemblies 148
assertiveness 85

Baker, Mike 36
Balfour, Lord 32
behaviour 20, 42, 62, 63
Bell, David 39
Bentham, Jeremy 127
Bible, the 30
Blair, Tony 40, 54
Blunkett, David 55
bog-standard 39
boundaries 122
Brown vs the Board of Education 47
Bubb, Sue 190
Bush, George 47
Byres, Stephen 37

Callaghan, James 34
Cambridge University 29, 168
Cameron, David 39, 54
Campbell, Alasdair 39
carpentry 68

CfBT Education Trust 52
character 15, 142
Church, the 28, 29, 30
citizenship 43
city academies 37
Clarke, Charles 37
Coelho, Paulo 127
compassion 115
compulsory education 31
Connery, Sir Sean 141
conservatism 23, 35, 36
courage 79, 147, 165
craftsmen 28
cynicism 130

data 180
deferred gratification 96
deregulation 35
Descartes, René 22
detentions 158
DfE 18, 37
doctrine of the mean 65
duty 153

EBD 181
Eccles, Sir David 34
Education Act 45
education research 21
Eldon, Lord 31
emotional intelligence 10, 20
endurance 102
enlightenment 33
epistemic humility 106

epistemology 21
Eton 30
Every Child Matters 39, 54
evolutionary equilibrium 23
Excellence in Cities 37

familial resemblance, theory of 24–5
Finland 53
Fletcher, Joseph 116
Flew, Anthony 55
Fonz, the 177
formula funding 35
Forster, William Edward 31
fortitude 98
free schools 35, 53
French education 48
Fry, Stephen 10

German education 48
Godwin's Law 15
Gove, Michael 39
grammar schools 29, 30, 31, 32, 33
Great Debate, the 34
Greek education 42, 61
GTC 40
guilds 30

happiness 11
head teachers 34
Hippocrates 23
history of education 21, 27–49
history of UK education 29–41
Hitchens, Christopher 183
Hitler, Adolf 48
HMI 34
Hobbes, Thomas 99
Holland Park School 34
home-tutoring 28
hothousing 23
Hume, David 118

improving skills 136, 142
industrial revolution 30

INSET 189, 191, 198
inspiration 20
intellectual vacuum 59
international comparisons 53

Jefferson, Thomas 46
Jesuits 17
Jihad 80
Joseph, Sir Keith 36
justice 71

Kant, Immanuel 118
karma 73
Kelly, Ruth 37
Kohlberg, Lawrence 97
Kolbe, Maximillian 92

Labour, New 37
Latin 45
laziness 127
league tables 35, 37
legacy of history 13
liberalism 33, 35
Local Education Authorities 32, 35,
    36, 37
Lyceum 41

Marx, Karl 25, 33
Maslow's hierarchy of needs 140
men of gold, silver, bronze 33
Mill, John Stuart 23, 31, 88
modern education 32
Mole Man, The 8
Montessori method 57
Moore, G. E. 55
Morris, Estelle 37, 39
multiple intelligences 140

National Curriculum 34, 37
natural sciences 21
NEETs 52
Nietzsche, Friedrich 95, 101
No Child Left Behind 47

normalisation 28
NQTs 82
NVQ 34

observations 149
Ofsted 18–19, 37, 43
Oxford University 29, 34

parents 91, 95, 157
pettiness 133
phone calls 148
PISA 56
Plato 33, 44, 48, 106
policy 52
Poor Law 30
potential 11
priest classes 28
private education 49
privilege 28
professionalism 9, 16, 19, 90
pseudoscience 48
Pythagoras 17

Queen Christina of Sweden 22
quitting 155

rackets 55, 60
Raikes, Robert 30
Rand, Ayn 193
Reformation, the 30
relationships 111
religious education 34, 57
research 56
responsibility 15, 17
Robinson, Sir Ken 83
Roman education 45
Romans 27
Ruskin College 34

SATs 35
Schools Council 34, 36
seating plans 153
secondary modern 33

self-esteem 20
SEN 37
siege mentality 132
social sciences 21
socialisation 10, 28
Socrates 8, 22, 106
Sophists 44
Sparta 43
stakeholders 34
Statutes, Acts 30, 31, 32, 33
Sunday School Movement 30
Sweden 41

teacher workout 64
teaching qualifications 28
teaching styles 24–5
teaching vices 127
teaching, good 18
technical schools 33
TES 62
Thatcher, Margaret 34, 36, 37
Thomson, Hugh 92
Tomlinson, Mike 39, 54
trade unions 33, 34, 36, 40, 54
Tripartite education 34
trips 150
Trivium 29
Twitter 10

universal entitlement 33, 48
universities 29
values 16, 186, 187
vices 101
virtue ethics 62

White, Barry 117
Winchester 30
Wisdom 105
Wittgenstein, Ludwig 24–5
Woodhead, Chris 39
work/life balance 195

Youth Training Scheme 34